THE BATTLE OF WAVRE AND GROUCHY'S RETREAT

THE BATTLE OF WAVRE AND GROUCHY'S RETREAT

A STUDY OF AN OBSCURE PART OF
THE WATERLOO CAMPAIGN

By W. HYDE KELLY, R.E.

WITH MAPS AND PLANS

The Naval & Military Press Ltd

Published by

The Naval & Military Press Ltd
Unit 5 Riverside, Brambleside
Bellbrook Industrial Estate
Uckfield, East Sussex
TN22 1QQ England

Tel: +44 (0)1825 749494

www.naval-military-press.com
www.nmarchive.com

In reprinting in facsimile from the original, any imperfections are inevitably reproduced and the quality may fall short of modern type and cartographic standards.

AUTHOR'S PREFACE

So much has been written on the Waterloo Campaign that, even in the smallest details, nothing new can be revealed; but the dazzling magnitude of the great battle itself has obscured a part of the campaign which is seldom studied —the battle against Thielemann, and Grouchy's skilful retreat from Wavre.

I have chosen this tail-end of the campaign because little is known about it; because it serves useful lessons even for to-day; because the operations leading up to the battle round Wavre are of great interest; and because a campaign full of mistakes should be studied as carefully as a campaign free from error. From history we obtain experience, and experience teaches us how to act for the future. We learn how great men of old time fought their battles and managed their retreats; we see the reasons of their successes and their failures; and we should endeavour to make use of our lessons when our own time comes.

Not that Grouchy can be deemed a great soldier; nor can his part of the 1815 campaign be regarded as of prime importance in itself; but as showing the small trifles that mar great plans in their execution, as showing how little a thing will sometimes destroy the grandest conceptions, his operations from 16th June to the end of the month are well worthy of attention.

I might have employed my time more profitably had I chosen to work upon some more illustrious name than Grouchy's, or upon some more modern campaign of greater advantage to the war student of to-day; but I chose to bring forward an obscure page in the history of the most famous campaign, for in that history there is much that may still be laid to heart.

Great deeds deserve great critics, but, as Colonel Henderson wrote in his Preface to "Stonewall Jackson," "if we were to wait for those who are really qualified to deal with the achievements of famous captains, we should, as a rule, remain in ignorance of the lessons of their lives, for men of the requisite capacity are few in a generation." Man is not so fortunate that he can live in every period; and for knowledge he must go backwards to search in history. The statesman will read of the great quarrels between Charles I. and his Parliament, not because he would imitate either the one side or the other, but because he will desire to mould future action upon the experience of the past. Napoleon himself prepared all his ambitious schemes from the pages of Tacitus, Plutarch and Livy, and the histories of the deeds of Hannibal, Alexander, and Cæsar. Wellington "made it a rule to study for some hours every day"; and since these two great men advocate study of history, who is there who shall gainsay the advantages of learning? But the true method of reading history requires something far deeper than mere perusal: it must be accompanied by careful and continuous thought. A true history will encourage the reader to bury himself in the very atmosphere of the time, and will bring him to see with his eyes the comings and goings of great men, the rights and wrongs of their deeds, and their impress upon contemporary people.

This small volume attempts nothing of this kind: it is a sketch, a mere outline, of a minor portion of a remarkable campaign. In it I have made no mention of the tactical formations employed; I have given no details of armaments, equipments, or means of transport; for these are now of no value to the soldier-student. The comments or remarks are to be taken or left, as it shall please the reader: they are my own views; possibly they may coincide with the views of others; in that case they will be interesting.

I may admit that these pages were at first written for my own use—mere notes taken down while I read a dozen authorities on the subject. I afterwards persuaded myself that my studies might prove of use to those who had little time to search the volumes in the libraries.

I trust I shall not offend German susceptibilities by omitting the prefix "von" in the Prussian names and titles. I only do so to save space.

I have to add my gratitude to the numerous writers and historians who have told the splendid story of Waterloo, and from whom I have drawn my facts.

W. HYDE KELLY.

August 1905.

CONTENTS

CHAP.		PAGE
I.	BRIEF DISCUSSION OF THE EARLIER OPERATIONS—UP TO LIGNY	1
II.	THE THIRD PRUSSIAN CORPS AND GROUCHY'S FORCES	52
III.	THE RETREAT OF THIELEMANN'S CORPS FROM SOMBREFFE	66
IV.	GROUCHY'S PURSUIT OF THE PRUSSIANS	80
V.	BLUCHER MARCHES TOWARDS MONT ST JEAN WITH THE FIRST, SECOND, AND FOURTH CORPS	100
VI.	THIELEMANN'S INSTRUCTIONS AND HIS DISPOSITIONS AT WAVRE	108
VII.	THE BATTLE OF WAVRE	115
VIII.	GROUCHY'S RETREAT	133
IX.	NOTES AND COMMENTS	153
	INDEX	165

MAPS

		PAGE
1. ILLUSTRATING THE OPERATIONS OF 15TH-20TH JUNE	. .	1
2. THE BATTLE OF WAVRE—POSITIONS AT DAYBREAK, 19TH JUNE		115
3. ILLUSTRATING GROUCHY'S RETREAT FROM NAMUR	. .	133

MAP ILLUSTRATING THE OPERA

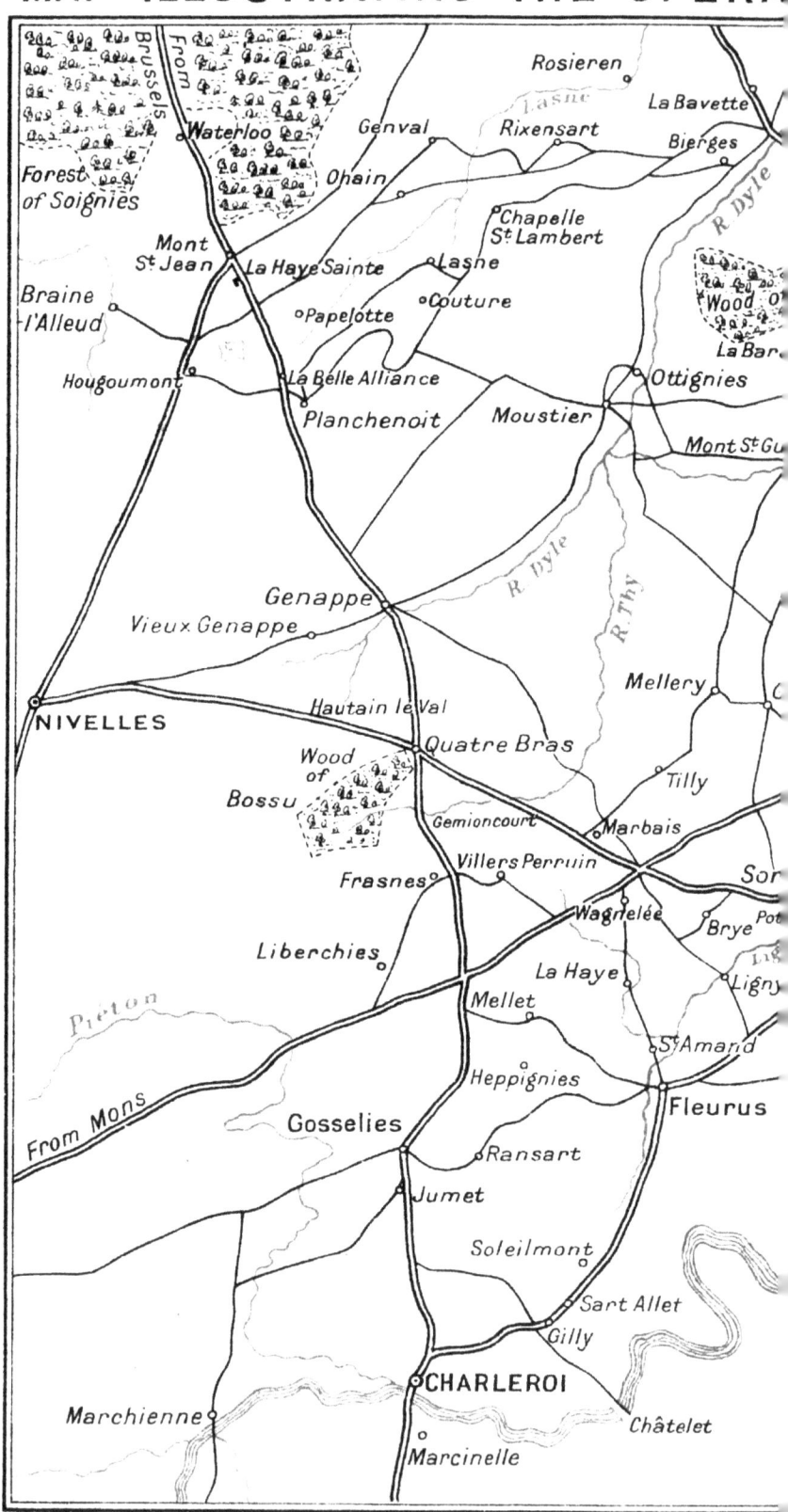

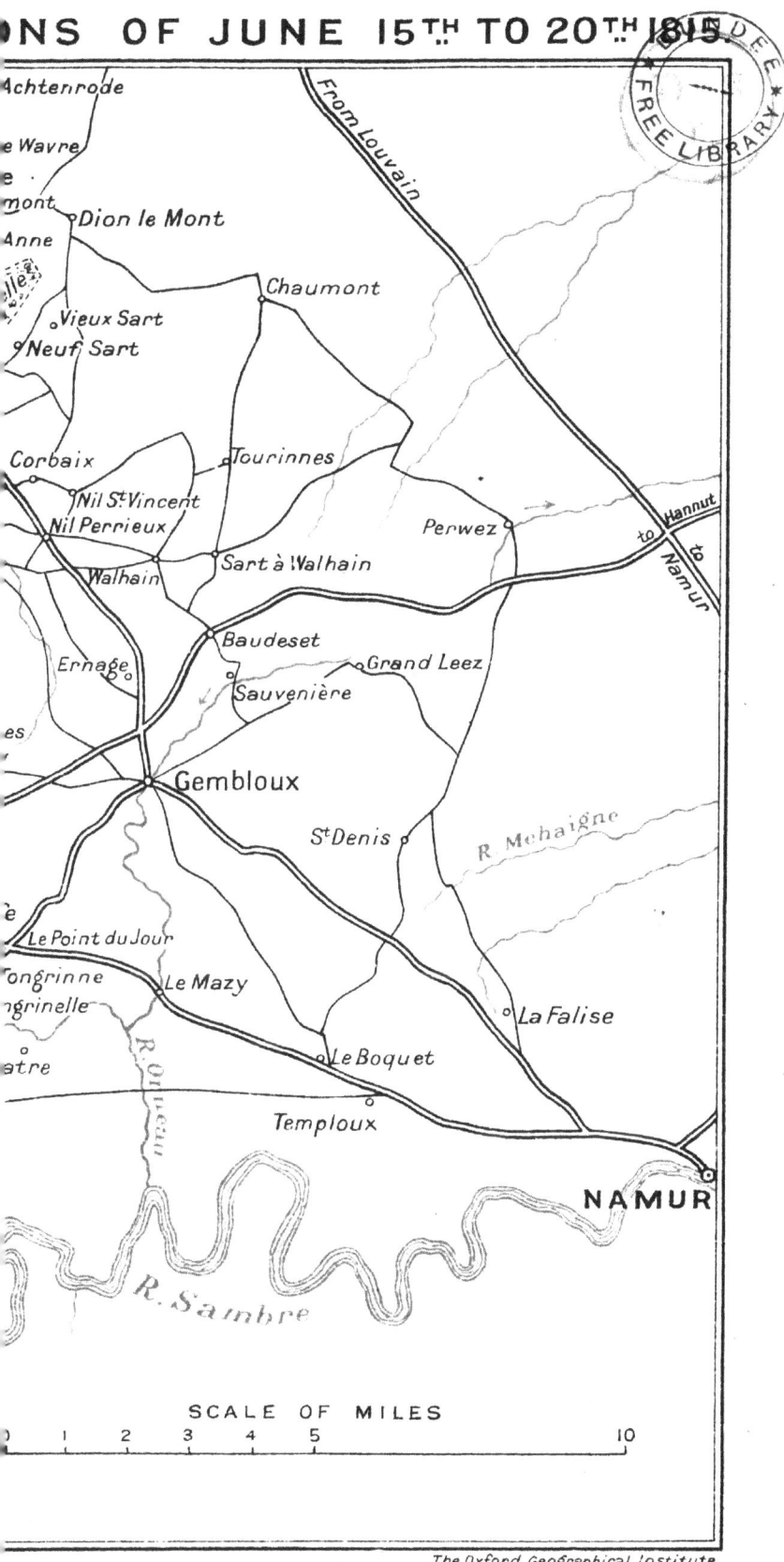

THE BATTLE OF WAVRE AND GROUCHY'S RETREAT

CHAPTER I

BRIEF DISCUSSION OF THE EARLIER OPERATIONS—UP TO LIGNY

THE Allied troops in the Netherlands had begun to concentrate as early as the 15th of March. They were cantoned from Trèves and Coblentz to Courtrai. But their commanders were away in Vienna — both Wellington and Blucher. The largest number that could be concentrated to meet a sudden attack on Belgium in April was 80,000 men. Of these, 23,000 were Anglo-Hanoverian troops, 30,000 were Prussians, 14,000 were Saxons, and the remainder Dutch-Belgians. The spirit of discipline was almost wholly wanting among the Saxons and Dutch-Belgians; the greater part of them had, at one time or another, served Napoleon, and were not to be trusted.

Kleist, commanding the Prussians on the Rhine, had arranged with the Prince of Orange, who commanded the troops in the Netherlands, that, in the event of a French attack, they would retire together on Tirlemont; thus leaving Brussels exposed, and giving the enemy a firm footing in Belgium.

By the 1st of April, Napoleon could have mustered a force of 50,000 men on the frontier near Charleroi. He could have marched direct on Brussels (as the Prince of Orange and Kleist had agreed to fall back). With Brussels in his hands, he could have turned and repeated his favourite strategy by falling upon the allied armies in turn. Wellington was dreading such an attack.

But the project, although it may have entered Napoleon's thoughts, was never seriously contemplated by him. His army, although rapidly being raised, organised, and equipped in hundreds of thousands of men, was not yet in a condition to enter upon a prolonged campaign. He might gain a slight temporary success with these 50,000 men; he might be reinforced by another 100,000 in the North; but, meantime, how should he check the other great invading armies of the Allies? For their preparations were forging ahead. Barclay de Tolly was marching with 167,000 Russians in three columns through

Germany. Marshal Schwarzenberg, commanding an Austrian army of 50,000 men, and the Archduke Ferdinand, at the head of 40,000 men, were hastening to reach the Rhine. One hundred and twenty thousand men were being collected in Lombardy, after Murat's decisive overthrow. Prince Wrede, commanding a Bavarian army 80,000 strong, was assembling his forces behind the Upper Rhine. Truly a formidable array!

To strike a premature blow at Belgium with 50,000 men did not therefore commend itself to Napoleon as a possible opening. By waiting, he not only increased his army and reserve forces; he made it appear that the war was being forced upon him by the threatened invasion of France. His apparent reluctance to open hostilities would be a great point in his favour. Then, again, the plans of the Allies would unfold themselves presently, and he could strike at will.

While the Allies were planning and re-planning, discussing and arguing their plans of campaign, their brilliant adversary was growing daily stronger. But the position was an intricate one. A too-hasty invasion of France with ill-concentrated forces would have brought about a repetition of the 1814 campaign outside Paris. There were to be no half-measures with Napoleon this time.

Many plans were put forward by the Allied generals; and after lengthy discussion, it was finally decided to adopt a modified scheme proposed by Schwarzenberg, which was to come into operation towards the end of July. This plan provided for the simultaneous invasion of France by six armies. Wellington, with 92,000 British, Dutch-Belgians, Hanoverians, Nassauers and Brunswickers, was to cross the frontier between Beaumont and Maubeuge; Blucher, with 116,000 Prussians, between Beaumont and Givet; Barclay de Tolly, with 150,000 Russians, *viâ* Saarlouis and Saarbruck; and Schwarzenberg, with 205,000 men — Austrians, Wurtembergers and Bavarians — by Basle; Frimont, with 50,000 Austrians and Piedmontese, was to advance on Lyons from Lombardy, while Bianchi, at the head of 25,000 Austrians, was to make for Provence. The first four armies were to converge on Paris, by Peronne, Laon, Nancy and Langres respectively; and the two last were to create a diversion in the South and support the Royalists.

This was the final plan of the Allies; but long before the date fixed for the first moves, Napoleon was fully acquainted with their designs. Newspaper reports and secret letters had kept him informed throughout the preparations. He tells us that he worked out two alternative plans of campaign. His first idea was to concentrate a force of 200,000 men outside Paris, and await the approach of the Allied armies. He proposed to gather the First, Second, Third, Fourth, Fifth and Sixth Corps, the Imperial Guard, and Grouchy's Cavalry Reserve, round the Capital, which would be garrisoned by 80,000 regular troops, mobilised guards and sharpshooters, strongly entrenched and governed by Davoût: and to concentrate round Lyons Suchet's army of the Alps, 23,000 men, and Lecourbe's Corps of the Jura, 8,000 men. All the great fortresses were strongly garrisoned; and Napoleon intended to let the Allies advance until they were surrounded with these powerful garrisons and faced by himself with 200,000 men. The date fixed by the Allies for the crossing of the frontier was 1st July. It would take them three weeks to draw near Paris. By that time the entrenchments round the Capital would be completed. But the Allies, operating on six different lines, would be obliged to detach large forces to watch Suchet and Lecourbe, and to mask the great strongholds in their way. When they had approached Paris, their great armies would have been thus reduced to 400,000 men, far from their bases, and faced by the greatest soldier of modern time. The campaign of 1814 would be repeated, but Napoleon would have 200,000 men at his back, and a powerful entrenched camp at Paris. Thus the Allies would in all probability be crushed in detail; whether they would recover and overwhelm Napoleon by sheer weight of numbers seemed doubtful.

But to allow France to be over-run in the meantime by the invaders would enrage the Parisians; and Parisians had always to be reckoned in any plan of Napoleon's. A more splendid scheme soon presented itself to him. He had a great idea of the importance of winning Brussels: and defensive warfare was unworthy of his genius. He resolved to attack before the Allies should be concentrated. By the middle of June his available forces on the Northern frontier would amount to 125,000 men.

"He would enter Belgium: he would beat in turn, or separately, the English and the Prussians; then, as soon as new reinforcements had arrived from the depôts, he would effect a junction with the 23,000 men under Rapp, and would bear down upon the Austro-Russians."[1]

Here was a plan after his own heart. To establish himself once more at the head of the nation he must win a glorious victory for France.

[1] Houssaye.

The minds of Frenchmen were peculiarly susceptible to the inspiriting effects of military glory. Therefore he would strike at Belgium: he would separate Blucher from Wellington and beat each army in turn. And here is revealed the nicety of his calculations. He must attack and beat either Wellington or Blucher before they could join their forces.

"If he directed his line of operations against Brussels through Ath, and debouched from Lille or Condé against Wellington's right, he would merely drive the English army towards the Prussian army, and two days later he would find himself face to face with their united forces. If, on the contrary, he marched against Blucher's left, through Givet and the valley of the Meuse, in the same way he would still hasten the union of the hostile forces by driving the Prussians to the English. Inspired by one of his finest strategical conceptions, the Emperor resolved to break boldly into the very centre of the enemy's cantonments, at the very point where the English and Prussians would probably concentrate. The road from Charleroi to Brussels forming the line of contact between the two armies, Napoleon, passing through Beaumont and Phillippeville, resolved, by this road, to fall like a thunderbolt on his foe."[1]

Wellington's troops were scattered in cantonments stretching over an arc from Oudenarde to Quatre-Bras. The Second Corps, under Lord

---

[1] Houssaye.

Hill, formed the extreme right, and occupied Ghent, Oudenarde, Ath and Leuze. The Corps was 27,000 strong, of whom scarcely 7,000 were British troops. The First Corps, under the Prince of Orange, occupied Mons, Rouelx, Soignies, Genappe, Seneffe, Frasnes, Braine-le-Comte, and Enghien. This Corps was 30,000 strong, of whom only 6,300 were British. Its left rested on Genappe, Quatre-Bras, and Frasnes, and was in touch with the right of the First Corps, of the Prussian army, under Zieten, whose headquarters were at Charleroi. Wellington's Reserve, 25,500 men, was posted in the neighbourhood of Brussels, under the Duke's personal command. The Cavalry, under Lord Uxbridge, was comprised in seven brigades, British and King's German Legion; with one Hanoverian brigade, five squadrons of Brunswick Cavalry, and three brigades of Dutch-Belgian Cavalry. The Brunswickers were stationed near Brussels; the three Dutch-Belgian brigades were allotted to the First Corps, and the remainder of the cavalry were stationed at Ninove, Grammont, and in the villages scattered along the Dender.

Wellington was expecting an attack by way of Lille and Courtrai, and always regarded this direction as Napoleon's best move. For his army was based on Ostend, Antwerp, and the sea;

hence, had Napoleon attacked by way of Mons, he would have cut Wellington's communications, and forced him to evacuate Brussels. On the other hand, he would have driven the English army towards the Prussians.

Wellington's dispositions were eminently suited to rapid concentration on threatened points, while, at the same time, they were sufficiently scattered to make the subsistence of the troops possible. He had selected Oudenarde, Ath, Enghien, Soignies, Nivelles, and Quatre-Bras as points of interior concentration; and in this way, by whichever route Napoleon chose to attack, Wellington could bring his Reserve to the threatened point, and at the same time bring the remainder of his forces into concentration, enabling him to throw at least two-thirds of his whole force in front of the enemy within twenty-four hours.

Blucher's army, 116,000 strong, was divided into four Corps. The First Corps, under Zieten, had its headquarters at Charleroi; and its outposts stretched from Bonne Espérance through Lobbes, Thuin and Gerpinnes to Sossoye. Its right was in touch with the left of the Prince of Orange's Corps of Wellington's army. The Second Corps, under Pirch I., had its headquarters at Namur. Its Divisions were stationed in Thorembey les Beguignes, Heron, Huy and

Hannut. Its outposts stretched from Sossoye to Dinant. The Third Corps, under Thielemann, whose headquarters were at Ciney, had its Divisions stationed at Asserre, Ciney, Dinant and Huy. Its outposts extended from Dinant to Rochefort. The Fourth Corps, Bulow's, had its headquarters at Liège: its Divisions were stationed at Warème, Hologne, Liers, Tongres and Lootz.

Blucher's scheme of concentration enabled him to collect his four Corps together at their respective points of assembly—Fleurus, Namur, Ciney and Liège, within twelve hours. If the French crossed the Sambre at Charleroi, Blucher intended to concentrate his army in front of Sombreffe, on the Namur-Nivelles road, where he would be within 8 miles of Quatre-Bras, Wellington's point of concentration under those circumstances. If Napoleon moved along the Meuse towards Namur, the First, Second and Fourth Corps were to concentrate on Namur, while Thielemann's Corps, the Third, acting from Ciney, would attack the enemy's right flank. If, again, Napoleon advanced on Ciney, Zieten, Pirch I. and Thielemann were to concentrate their Corps on Ciney, and the Fourth Corps was to remain at Liège as a Reserve.

These were the dispositions of the Allies; but

they were not strategically in a sound position. Wellington's line of supply lay through Ostend and Antwerp to the sea; Blucher's lay by Liège and Maestricht to the Rhine. Therefore, in the event of a disaster to either, or both, their lines of retreat would carry them further apart. It was this weakness on which Napoleon based his whole plan. The Prussian army, being the nearer to Napoleon, would be the first met with, and therefore the first to concentrate. By a rapid crossing of the Sambre at Charleroi, Napoleon would force the First Corps back on Fleurus, where the Prussian army was to concentrate, and throw himself on the point of junction of the Allied armies when concentrated; namely, the Quatre-Bras - Sombreffe road. He knew that the Prussians, by reason of their dispositions, would be concentrated first, and he therefore hoped, by possessing himself of the point of junction, to beat their concentrated army before Wellington, who, he decided, would be much slower in assembling his troops, could come up to Quatre-Bras. It was of vital importance to Napoleon to beat the Prussian army, entirely and completely, in its position at Sombreffe, before Wellington could come to Blucher's assistance. The retreat of the Prussians on Wavre without such a decisive defeat, would have upset the whole plan: for

Wellington would then have retired and united with Blucher, either in front of Brussels or behind it. But, if thoroughly beaten, the Prussians would retreat on Liège: and only in this way could Napoleon effectually separate the two armies and crush them in turn. Such was Napoleon's argument. In conception, the plan was brilliant; but its execution was unworthy of him.

Composition of the French Army.

Napoleon's Grand army for the invasion of Belgium was made up of the First, Second, Third, Fourth and Sixth Corps d'Armée; four Corps of Reserve Cavalry; and the Imperial Guard; a total of 116,124 men. The First Corps, under d'Erlon, consisted of the First, Second, Third, and Fourth Infantry Divisions, and the First Light Cavalry Division. In the early part of June, the Corps was stationed at Lille. The Second Corps, under Reille, consisted of the Fifth, Sixth, Seventh and Eighth Infantry Divisions, and the Second Light Cavalry Division. This Corps was quartered at Valenciennes. The Third Corps, Vandamme's, comprised the Ninth, Tenth, and Eleventh Infantry Divisions, and the Third Light Cavalry Division, and was stationed at Mézières. The Fourth Corps, Gérard's, was composed of the

Twelfth, Thirteenth and Fourteenth Infantry Divisions, and the Seventh Light Cavalry Division. The Corps was stationed in Metz, Longwy, and Thionville. The Sixth Corps, Lobau's, was made up of the Nineteenth, Twentieth, and Twenty-first Infantry Divisions; it was stationed at Laon. Grouchy commanded the four Corps of Reserve cavalry; these First, Second, Third, and Fourth Cavalry Corps were commanded by Pajol, Excelmans, Kellermann, and Milhaud respectively; they were mostly stationed between the river Aisne and the frontier. The Imperial Guard consisted of twelve regiments of infantry, two regiments of heavy cavalry, three of light cavalry, and thirteen batteries of artillery. The Guard left Paris for Avesnes early in June. To the First and Second Corps d'Armée were attached six batteries; to the Third and Fourth, five batteries; and to the Sixth, four batteries of artillery.

This army was the best, in point of courage, warlike spirit, and devotion to himself, that Napoleon ever led. But the men were without discipline, and distrusted their leaders. Napoleon's generals were not the best that had ever served under him. Ney was a tried veteran, the "bravest of the brave," but he had just come over to Napoleon from Louis XVIII. Grouchy had never held an independent command. It is remarkable that *both* Ney and Grouchy should have failed Napoleon in this, his last, campaign; but neither were fitted to the great trusts committed to them. Napoleon himself was not the same man who had beaten back the Allies a year previously at Montmirail, Montereau, and Champaubert, but he was still a master of strategy and the strongest man of France.

The First Movements of the French.

Napoleon began his concentration early in June. He moved the First Corps from Lille to Avesnes; the Second from Valenciennes to Maubeuge; the Third from Mézières to Chimay; the Fourth from Thionville to Rocroi; the Sixth from Laon to Avesnes; and the Guard from Paris to Avesnes.

The concentration was in full swing, with the exception of Grouchy's Reserve Cavalry, when Napoleon left Paris on the night of 11th June. Grouchy had not received his orders for concentration from Soult, the Chief of the Staff, who had neglected to send them until the 12th. Here was an omission at the outset which might well have had serious results. But Grouchy lost no time in setting his Corps on their roads, and by rapid marching he had all his cavalry beyond Avesnes on the night of the 13th.

On the evening of the 14th Napoleon moved his headquarters to Beaumont. The First Corps was on the extreme left, between Maubeuge and Solre-sur-Sambre; the Second Corps between Solre-sur-Sambre and Leers; the Third and Sixth Corps between Beaumont and the Sambre; the Fourth Corps between Phillippeville and Florenne; Grouchy's Reserve Cavalry between Beaumont and Phillippeville; the Imperial Guard at Beaumont. This concentration was brilliantly planned, and skilfully executed: worthy of Napoleon's best days.

The French army crossed the frontier early in the morning of the 15th of June, in three columns. The left column (d'Erlon's and Reille's Corps) crossed by Thuin and Marchienne; the centre column (Vandamme's, Lobau's Corps, Imperial Guard, and Grouchy's Reserve Cavalry), at whose head was the Emperor himself, crossed by Ham-sur-Heure, Jamioux, and Marcinelle; the right column, Gérard's Corps, by Florennes and Gerpinnes. The front was covered by twelve regiments of cavalry.

The arrangements for relieving the troops of a fatiguing march by avoiding the crossing of columns in front of each other, and for the communication between each column, were admirable. The baggage and ammunition waggons, except those of the latter which were required for immediate use, were kept 9 miles in rear of the army. The advanced guards of the different columns communicated constantly with each other, so that no column should get ahead of the others. A screen of scouts was sent out in all directions to obtain every scrap of information as to the enemy's position, and report direct to the Emperor. Everything was to be done to ensure the rapid march of a well-concentrated army on the point where it was expected that the Prussians would be met with. But three of the Corps commanders failed to carry out their instructions. D'Erlon started from his camp at half-past four instead of at three o'clock, as ordered. Vandamme never knew of the march of the army until Lobau's Corps pushed on his rear: the orders sent to him from headquarters had not reached him, owing to an accident to the officer sent by Soult. And Gérard, who should have marched at three, did not reach Florennes until 7 A.M. All this was carelessness. Soult should have sent such important orders in duplicate. It is interesting to observe how these delays affected the subsequent movements of the columns on the 15th.

But, first of all, the centre column shall be followed, as being that led by the Emperor himself. In the advance on Charleroi, Pajol's cavalry led the way. Zieten's outposts were everywhere driven in, and when Pajol entered Charleroi at midday (the 15th) the Prussians had withdrawn, and taken up a strong position at Gilly, 2 miles north-east of Charleroi. The centre column halted to await Vandamme's arrival; for Grouchy, who did not like the appearance of the Prussian position, would not attack until he had Excelman's Cavalry and Vandamme's Corps with him. Napoleon, impatient at the delay, took command in person at 5 P.M., and pushed home a vigorous attack; and the Prussians retired at dusk to Fleurus. Vandamme and the Cavalry bivouacked within 2 miles of the Prussians. The Guard bivouacked between Gilly and Charleroi; Lobau's Corps south of the river, near Charleroi; and Gérard's Corps on the right, crossing the Sambre at Châtelet, bivouacked on the road to Fleurus. Napoleon thus had the Third, Fourth, and Sixth Corps, the Imperial Guard, and Grouchy's Cavalry concentrated between Fleurus and Charleroi, intending to attack the Prussians in strength next day, either at Fleurus or at Sombreffe. The Emperor passed the night at Charleroi.

Had it not been for Vandamme's delay, and had Grouchy attacked the Prussians at once at Gilly, the latter could have pushed his enemy as far as Sombreffe that night, which it was Napoleon's intention that he should have done. But Vandamme's slowness prevented Grouchy from advancing further than Fleurus that evening.

On the Left, matters had not, by nightfall, progressed as far as Napoleon wished. Reille, in accordance with his instructions, had marched with his Corps, the Second, from Leers at 3 A.M., and pushed on to Marchienne, everywhere driving back the enemy's outposts. He was then ordered to march on Gosselies, where it was reported that a body of Prussians were in position. He therefore pushed on his troops along the Charleroi-Brussels road; and finding Jumet occupied by a Prussian rearguard, he drove out the enemy, and reached Gosselies at about 5 P.M. Marshal Ney now arrived on the scene, and, having just come from the Emperor, from whom he received his orders, took over the command of the Left Wing. Ney pushed on to Frasnes with Piré's Cavalry and Bachelu's Infantry Division: Girard's Division was sent to pursue the Prussians, who had retreated from Gosselies towards Fleurus: the remaining divisions of Reille's Corps—Jerome's and Foy's—stayed at Gosselies. Ney drove back

Saxe-Weimar's Brigade from Frasnes at 6.30 P.M.; the brigade retiring on Quatre-Bras. Lefebvre-Desnouette's Division of Light Cavalry of the Guard had arrived with Ney, and was now moved in support of his infantry at Frasnes.

Thus Ney, at 6.30 P.M., while there were still nearly three hours of daylight left, had with him two light cavalry divisions, and one infantry division, at Frasnes. The distance to Quatre-Bras was $2\frac{1}{2}$ miles. In less than an hour he could have reached the cross-roads and attacked Saxe-Weimar's Brigade. But he merely pushed his cavalry forward, reconnoitred the position, and then withdrew his men to Frasnes, himself returning to Gosselies at about 8.30 P.M.

Now it has been fiercely contested that Ney received verbal orders from Napoleon to occupy Quatre-Bras on the night of the 15th. Whether he did or did not is a point still undecided by the authorities on the campaign, but it matters little, for Napoleon, in his written orders to Ney on the 16th, expressed his satisfaction with the progress of the night before, and did not blame Ney for his failure to occupy the cross-roads. As a matter of fact, Saxe-Weimar made such a bold show of resistance to the reconnaissance sent by Ney, that the latter was entirely deceived as to his enemy's numbers: he believed that the

English were in great force there. Had Ney attacked Quatre-Bras that night, he would have driven back Saxe-Weimar's Brigade of Nassauers, the only troops in occupation, and seized the most important point in the theatre of war. But, viewing the question from what must have been Ney's own point of view, he was acting on sound strategical principles by not pushing ahead too far. He had only just arrived on the ground, and was not acquainted with any of his Staff, or his divisional generals, or even with the strength of his troops. He believed that a strong English force held Quatre-Bras, and that, by attacking, he would be overwhelmed by the whole of Wellington's army; that Napoleon's Left Wing would be crushed. He therefore adopted more cautious methods, and awaited the arrival of d'Erlon's Corps, and news of the progress of the Centre and Right Wing.

Prince Bernard of Saxe-Weimar may be credited with having saved the situation for the Allies. Had he adhered rigidly to the principles of strategy, he would have fallen back from Quatre-Bras; but instead, his fine courage prompted him to hold on until supports should arrive, and his boldness triumphed over Ney's prudence. If Ney had seized Quatre-Bras that night, and if the succeeding events had taken place as they did take place, the battle of Waterloo would never have been fought, for Wellington could not have risked a battle without hope of Prussian assistance. But there were many little risks and chances which might have changed the whole result of the campaign!

To return to d'Erlon. By starting an hour and a half later than he was ordered to do, he lost most valuable time; and throughout the day he took no pains to make up for the delay, although he actually received an order from Soult, late in the afternoon, to the effect that he was to join Reille at Gosselies that evening. Instead of this, by nightfall his leading division, Durutte's, was at Jumet, 1½ miles in rear of Gosselies, and his Headquarters at Marchienne, 6 miles in rear! Matters had not progressed at all satisfactorily on the Left Wing.

The 15th of June on the side of the Allies.

Blucher had decided upon a concentration of his whole army at Sombreffe, in the event of Napoleon attacking by Charleroi. Therefore, on the evening of the 14th, he ordered the Second, Third, and Fourth Corps to concentrate on Sombreffe, while the First Corps was to make a stout resistance, and fall back slowly on Fleurus, which Zieten was to hold, in order to gain time for the concentration. These arrangements were made without any definite agreement between Wellington and Blucher, as to the Duke's movements under these circumstances. It was understood that each should give the other all the assistance in his power, in the event of a French attack; but no formal undertaking for definite action was entered into. Besides, Blucher, when he ordered his concentration, believed that Wellington's troops were too scattered to allow of their concentration within two days. He could not therefore have expected much actual support from Wellington. There was also the possibility that Wellington himself was confronted with a strong force.

In the concentration of the Prussian Corps, another defect in the transmission and execution of orders from Headquarters must be mentioned. Gneisenau, the chief of Blucher's Staff, sent instructions to Bulow, commanding the Fourth Corps, on the 14th, to the effect that he was so to dispose his Corps that his troops might reach Hannut in one march. The order was indefinite, and contained no statement that Napoleon was about to attack; there was no mention of the disposition of the other Prussian Corps; no mention of Blucher's intentions, or of the general situation. This was culpable negligence on the part of the chief of the Staff. It was his duty under the circumstances to transmit all such important information to all the Corps commanders; and because Bulow's Corps was some distance in rear, is no reason why such a necessary step should have been omitted. The result was a serious delay on the part of the Fourth Corps. At midnight on the 14th, a second despatch from Gneisenau was sent to Bulow, ordering a concentration of his Corps on Hannut. The first despatch reached Bulow at 5 A.M. on the 15th, when he was at Liège. The instructions contained in it were at once acted upon, and Bulow sent a report to this effect to Headquarters. While these instructions were being carried out, the second despatch arrived towards midday (on the 15th). Its contents seemed to Bulow to be impossible to act upon until the next day, for most of his troops were by this time so far in their movement that the new order could not reach them in time to be carried out that night; also there would be no quarters prepared for those troops which were still within reach of the new instructions. Futhermore, this second despatch was also indefinite. It contained no positive order that Bulow was to move his headquarters to Hannut; it merely suggested that Hannut appeared suitable. There was no mention of the commencement of hostilities. Bulow therefore decided to postpone the execution of this order until the 16th, and he sent a report to this effect to Blucher, promising to be in Hannut by noon next day (16th). The officer sent with this report reached Namur at 9 P.M., expecting to find Blucher there, but he discovered that Headquarters had been removed to Sombreffe. Meanwhile, a third despatch was sent off at 11 A.M. on the 15th from Namur, instructing Bulow to move the Fourth Corps, after a rest at Hannut, on Gembloux, starting at daybreak on the 16th. The orderly carrying this message naturally went to Hannut, where he expected to find Bulow. At Hannut he found Gneisenau's second despatch lying unopened, awaiting Bulow's arrival. He then started off at all speed with both despatches to Liège, where he arrived at daybreak on the 16th. But by this time Gneisenau's instructions were impracticable. Thus Bulow, through no fault of his own, was prevented from reaching the field of Ligny with his Corps, when his arrival on the right flank of the French might have had the same effect that the arrival of the Prussian army had at the great battle two days later.

While the concentration of the Second and Third Corps was rapidly progressing behind him,

Zieten was occupied with his retreat on Fleurus. At half-past three in the morning of the 15th, the Prussian picquets in front of Lobbes, a village on the Sambre, were driven in by the advanced guard of the French Left Column (this was the head of Reille's Corps advancing). An hour later, the French opened with artillery on Maladrie, a hamlet about a mile in front of Thuin. It was this cannonade which was heard by the troops of Steinmetz's Division in Fontaine l'Evêque, and even Zieten at Charleroi heard it. He therefore lost no time in sending reports to both Blucher and Wellington that fighting had actually commenced. His report to Wellington gave the Duke definite news that an attack on Charleroi was imminent, but it did not induce him to alter his plans in any way. For Wellington was still apprehensive of an attack by way of Mons, and he judged that his army was in the best position to meet such an attack. He was unwilling to engage himself in a move eastwards while there was a chance of the French attacking from the westwards. With such a belief, it is clear that Wellington, by concentrating prematurely at Quatre-Bras, which it was his intention to do if Napoleon's attack should eventually be by the Charleroi-Brussels road, would merely carry out the very move which his enemy would wish. Therefore he awaited more definite news of the French attack on Zieten.

But Zieten's report to Blucher made the Marshal more than ever assured of the wisdom of concentrating at Sombreffe.

The retreat of Zieten's Corps was very ably carried out. The Prussians at Maladrie, after maintaining a stubborn resistance, were finally overpowered, but they retreated in good order on Thuin. Here they joined a battalion of Westphalian Landwehr, and resistance was made until 7 A.M., when, after suffering very heavy losses, the Prussians fell back to Montigny. Here, again, they joined two squadrons of Dragoons, who covered the rest of their retreat to Marchienne. But the French cavalry, under Pajol, pushed on so vigorously, and the small retreating column suffered such severe losses, that, upon arrival at Marchienne, a mere skeleton was left. By this time also the outposts at Lobbes had effected their retreat on Marchienne. General Steinmetz, commanding the First Division of Zieten's Corps, was now fully aware of the French attack. He therefore sent a staff officer to warn Van Merlen, who commanded the Dutch-Belgian outposts at St. Symphorien between Binche and Mons, and to inform him that he was falling back with his Division upon Charleroi.

The manner in which the outposts fell back, and the readiness with which reports as to the enemy's movements and those of the several Prussian picquets and supports were passed from one part of the retreating Division to the other, and from the right of Zieten's corps to the left of Wellington's army, are worthy of the closest attention. The Prussian commanders thoroughly understood the value of rapid and accurate information, distributed to all parts of their commands. The long Napoleonic wars had taught them something of their profession.

Zieten's management of his retreat marks him as a very capable soldier. Towards 8 A.M. he satisfied himself that the whole French army was making for Charleroi. He therefore sent out the following orders for retreat: the First Division (Steinmetz's) to retire by Courcelles to Gosselies, and take up a position behind the village; the Second Division to gain time for the retreat of the First by defending the bridges over the Sambre at Châtelet, Charleroi, and Marchienne; it was then to fall back behind Gilly. The Third and Fourth Divisions, with the cavalry and artillery reserves, were to take up position at Fleurus.

Meanwhile, Napoleon was pushing rapidly on Charleroi with the Imperial Guard and Pajol's

Cavalry Corps. The Prussian detachment holding the bridge connecting Marcinelle and Charleroi made a stout defence, but was soon overpowered, and by noon the French had obtained possession of the town. The Third and Fourth Divisions of Zieten's Corps were by this time well on the road to Fleurus, but Steinmetz's Division was in great jeopardy. For the French were already masters of the Sambre, even below Charleroi, and the First Division was in danger of being cut off from its retreat on Gosselies. Accordingly Zieten, with great resolution, detached three battalions of infantry from the Third Division, and sent them to Colonel Lutzow, who was holding Gosselies with a regiment of Lancers from Roder's Reserve Cavalry. Lutzow placed one battalion in Gosselies, and took up a position in reserve with the remainder. As soon as the French had taken Charleroi, Napoleon ordered Pajol to send a brigade of Light Cavalry towards Gosselies, and to take the remainder of his Corps towards Gilly. The Brigade actually reached Jumet ahead of Steinmetz's Division, which had not yet crossed a small stream called the Piéton, which ran between Fontaine l'Evêque and Gosselies. But Colonel Lutzow went out with his regiment of Lancers from Gosselies, met the French Hussars, and drove them back with loss, enabling Steinmetz to reach the village in safety.

In the meantime reinforcements, consisting of the advanced guard of Reille's Corps, were being pushed along the Gosselies road, with a view to cutting off Steinmetz's retreat, and separating Zieten's Corps from Wellington's army. This move of the French was very skilful, but Steinmetz, perceiving that his position was one of great danger, made a feint against the French left flank, and, covering his retreat with a regiment of Lancers and one of Hussars, withdrew to Heppignies, a village half-way between Gosselies and Fleurus. Had Steinmetz been caught and surrounded at Gosselies, Blucher would have been weaker by one Division in the great struggle at Ligny next day; and he could ill afford to reduce his numbers.

Ney, who had taken over the command of the French Left Wing, and who was at this time pushing on with Piré's Cavalry and Bachelu's Infantry to Frasnes, sent Girard's Division of Reille's Corps to pursue Steinmetz. Girard occupied Ransart, and made an attack upon Heppignies, but the Prussians drove him back, and retired in good order to Fleurus, thus rejoining the main body of their Corps, and effecting their retreat in a very skilful manner.

In the Prussian centre, meanwhile, Pirch II.'s Second Division, which had been ordered to gain time for the retreat of the First, retired to Gilly, on the road to Fleurus, when the French entered Charleroi. At Gilly the Prussians took up a strong position and prepared to delay the French advance as much as possible. Pirch's line of defence stretched from Soleilmont on his right, to Châtelineau on his left; and a small stream ran in his front at the foot of the ridge on which his position stood. His left flank was further strengthened by a detachment holding the bridge over the Sambre at Châtelet. Cavalry patrols watched the valley of the Sambre for the approach of Gérard's Corps, which was already marching on Châtelet. Had Gérard marched earlier from Phillippeville, he would have prevented, by his occupation of Châtelet earlier in the day, Pirch's stand at Gilly.

Grouchy had orders to take Vandamme's Corps and Excelmans' Cavalry, and pursue the Prussians along the Charleroi-Fleurus road; but he was deceived as to the strength of the enemy at Gilly. Fearing to attack without further reinforcements, he rode back to Napoleon for instructions. This was at about 5 P.M. Napoleon, fretting at the delay, which he regarded as needless, himself rode out with four squadrons of Cavalry of the Guard, and reconnoitred Pirch's position. He soon satisfied himself as to Pirch's real strength, and gave Grouchy orders to attack at once. Accordingly, at 6 P.M., artillery fire opened on the Prussians from two batteries; three infantry columns from Vandamme's Corps were ordered to assault in front, and two cavalry brigades to menace the Prussian flanks. Pirch was preparing to reply to the French artillery fire, when he received orders from Zieten to retire on Fleurus *viâ* Lambusart. As soon as he began to withdraw his battalions, the French cavalry, under Letort, made a vigorous attack. The Prussian infantry resisted stoutly, and a regiment of dragoons, with great boldness, charged the French squadrons with such effect that they were for the moment checked, and the Prussians were able to gain the cover of the wood of Fleurus. A battalion of the Sixth Regiment of the Line, by forming square repeatedly, bravely kept the enemy's cavalry at a distance, and gained very valuable time for the retreat of the rest of Pirch's Division. In front of Lambusart, where Pirch joined some battalions of the Third Division and Roder's Reserve Cavalry, a fresh position was taken up, and a regiment of Brandenburg Dragoons, sent by Zieten to support Pirch II., did excellent service by charging the

French horsemen and checking their pursuit. Towards eight o'clock three batteries of French Horse Artillery, which accompanied the cavalry, opened fire on Lambusart; but night was coming on, and the attack died out very shortly afterwards. Pirch II. then withdrew to Fleurus, where he joined the remainder of Zieten's Divisions, and the whole Corps retreated to Ligny. Steinmetz had reached Fleurus from Heppignies at about 10 P.M.

Zieten's retreat in the face of almost the whole French army is worthy of close attention. His men had been marching and fighting from three o'clock in the morning until ten o'clock at night, and had engaged the enemy in one or two very sharp conflicts. The skilful manner in which each Division was withdrawn without getting too closely engaged with the enemy, and in which the Divisions supported each other, is illustrative of the best methods of war. That he was able to concentrate his Corps at Fleurus with a loss of only 1,200 men, after having checked the rapid onset of the French, speaks very highly for Zieten's skill in generalship. The campaign of Waterloo still affords useful lessons and examples to modern students.

The Prussian Second Corps, under Pirch I., reached Sombreffe by ten o'clock at night; the

Third Corps passed the night at Namur; while the Fourth Corps was still near Liège.

On Wellington's side, Van Merlen, commanding the outposts between Mons and Binche, received the report from General Steinmetz at 8 A.M., to the effect that the French had attacked and driven in his outposts, and that he was falling back on Charleroi with his Division. Early in the morning the troops of Perponcher's Dutch-Belgian Division, which was stationed at Hautain-le-Val, Frasnes, and Villers Perruin, heard firing from the direction of Charleroi. In the afternoon, definite news reached them of the enemy's attack on Charleroi, and Perponcher at once assembled his First Brigade (Bylandt's) at Nivelles. A picquet of the Second Nassau battalion was posted in front of Frasnes to give warning of the French advance. In the meantime, Prince Bernard of Saxe Weimar, with his Brigade of Nassau troops, belonging to Perponcher's Division, on his own initiative moved forward from Genappe to Frasnes, reporting his action to the headquarters of his division at Hautain-le-Val; and Perponcher approved. When Ney advanced on Frasnes in the evening, with Piré's cavalry and Bachelu's infantry, Saxe Weimar, after making a determined show of resistance, skilfully withdrew behind Quatre-Bras, and Ney, as before-mentioned, was quite deceived as to his actual strength, and forebore to attack that night.

Zieten's report to Wellington, sent off from Charleroi at 5 A.M., reached the Duke's headquarters at Brussels at 9 A.M. Wellington did not consider the news sufficiently definite to cause him to make any immediate alteration in his dispositions. But at three o'clock in the afternoon, the Prince of Orange, coming from the outposts near Mons, where he had seen Van Merlen, and obtained information of the attack on the Prussians and of their retreat, reported his intelligence to the Duke. Wellington was now satisfied of the true direction of the French attack, but he sent orders to General Dornberg at Mons to report at once any movement of the French in that direction. He then ordered his troops to concentrate at their respective headquarters. On the left, Perponcher's and Chassé's Divisions were to assemble at Nivelles; the Third British Division (Alten's) was to concentrate at Braine-le-Comte and march on Nivelles in the night; the First British Division (Cooke's) was to assemble at Enghien. In the centre, Clinton's Division (the Second British) was to collect at Ath, and Colville's (the Fourth British) at Grammont. On the right, Steedman's Division and Anthing's Brigade of Dutch-Belgians were to march on Sotteghem. Uxbridge's cavalry was to assemble at Ninove, except Dornberg's Brigade, which was to march on Vilvorde; (still Wellington had apprehensions for his right). The Reserve was kept in readiness in and around Brussels; with orders to be prepared to march at once.

Late that night (the 15th), towards ten o'clock, news of Ney's attack at Frasnes was received by the Prince of Orange at Braine-le-Comte. The latter forwarded the report to Wellington, adding that Saxe Weimar had fallen back to Quatre-Bras, and that the French advance had been checked there. A despatch from Blucher at Namur also reached Wellington about this time, and the Duke decided to march his troops more to their left—*i.e.* towards the Prussians. He therefore issued a second batch of orders that night, directing Cooke's Division from Enghien to Braine-le-Comte; Clinton's and Colville's Divisions from Ath and Grammont to Enghien; and the cavalry from Ninove to Enghien. The other dispositions were to remain as they were.

At the close of the 15th, Napoleon's position promised success for his efforts next day. Blucher had only Zieten's Corps concentrated at Ligny; Pirch's Corps was still some miles back. Wellington's army was still far from Quatre-Bras. Surely, if Napoleon advanced to the attack of the Prussians at daybreak on the 16th, he must, with his overwhelming forces, crush half of Blucher's army and force the remainder to fall back on Liège? And Ney, if he attacked with Reille's and d'Erlon's Corps (for the latter might have pushed on during the night)—or even with Reille's Corps and Piré's Cavalry—could have driven back the English force at Quatre-Bras, which, by daybreak on the 16th, had only been reinforced by the remainder of Perponcher's Dutch-Belgian Division? Ney had ridden to Charleroi in the night, and had had an interview with Napoleon. He must, therefore, have known the state of affairs in the centre and on the right; he must have told Napoleon how matters stood on his wing. Why did not Napoleon order him to attack Quatre-Bras at daybreak on the 16th? There is no satisfactory answer. It is inconceivable that Napoleon, than whom no general has ever been bolder and more decisive in his moves or quicker to take action at critical moments, should have neglected to spend the night of the 15th in bringing up the troops in rear—Lobau's Corps, d'Erlon's Corps, Gérard's Corps. What if the columns had straggled out and become doubled in length? Had Napoleon's troops never made a greater effort in his earlier campaigns? There is no doubt existing that Napoleon, great warrior as he was, let his opportunity slip on the night of the 15th. His advanced troops were within 2 miles of Ligny, and 3 of the Quatre-Bras-Sombreffe road. Was not this the very point he had aimed at so carefully in his plan of campaign? He was already almost master of the line of junction of Wellington's and Blucher's armies. He had, in fact, almost, but not quite, attained the main objective of his scheme. It was within his grasp on the night of the 15th. How could Wellington prevent Ney from capturing Quatre-Bras at daybreak on the 16th? And how could Blucher save Ligny and Sombreffe, if Napoleon chose to bring up his two Corps from Charleroi and Châtelet, and attack at dawn with these overwhelming numbers? Both these attacks would have called for great efforts from the French troops, who had been marching and fighting since 3 A.M. on the 15th; but the attacks would have been finished in three or four hours, and *then* Napoleon could have thought of giving rest to his tired infantry, while his cavalry pursued the Prussians back towards Liège. A day spent in resting and in concentrating, and Napoleon could have turned to deal with Wellington. The Napoleon of Jena and Austerlitz would have won the campaign on the 15th.

But the delays of the 15th were insignificant in comparison with those of the 16th. And there were not only delays on the 16th, but very serious mistakes—although of a kind without which no war has ever been waged. It is not our intention to criticise these mistakes so much as to discuss their effects on the course of the campaign, and to illustrate their grievous results.

Movements on the 16th.

Ney, on his return to Gosselies from his interview with Napoleon, ordered Reille to move Jerome's and Foy's Divisions, with his five batteries of artillery, to Frasnes, whither he himself went. Ney's misgivings as to the wisdom of attacking Quatre-Bras were not unfounded. He feared a movement against his right flank by a strong force of Prussians whom he believed to be between Quatre-Bras and Ligny. He was anxious for his left flank, in case some of Wellington's troops were moving against him from the direction of Nivelles. He was ignorant of the real strength in front of him at Quatre-Bras. He had no staff officers whom he could send out to gather information on these points. He was unwilling to risk damaging Napoleon's plans by inviting defeat while so far in advance of the centre column. He therefore waited for d'Erlon's Corps and Kellermann's Corps of heavy cavalry, which Napoleon had promised to send him. He despatched orders to d'Erlon to bring up the First Corps with the utmost speed to Frasnes.

In the meantime, Wellington's troops were fast moving on Nivelles and Quatre-Bras. Lord Uxbridge's Cavalry and Clinton's Division were ordered to move on Braine-le-Comte, and Steedman's Division with Anthing's Brigade from Sotteghem to Enghien at daybreak. Picton's Division started from Brussels for Quatre-Bras at 2 A.M. The Duke of Brunswick, with 5,000 Brunswick infantry, left at 3 A.M. At 3 A.M. also Perponcher reached Quatre-Bras with his First Brigade of Dutch-Belgians, under Bylandt. The Prince of Orange arrived at Quatre-Bras at 6 A.M., reconnoitred Ney's position, and pushed Perponcher's troops further forward. He gave orders that as great a show of strength as possible was to be made, but a close or premature engagement with the enemy was to be avoided. Thus at 7 A.M. the Prince had 9 battalions of Dutch-Belgian troops, and 16 guns, holding Quatre-Bras; Ney opposite, with Piré's Division of Lancers, Bachelu's Division of Infantry, and Lefebvre-Desnouette's Cavalry of the Guard, in all 9,700 men, and the remainder of Reille's Corps in support at Frasnes!

Wellington himself arrived at Quatre-Bras at 11 A.M., inspected the position, saw that the French were not preparing an immediate attack, and complimented the Prince of Orange on his dispositions. He then rode off to the mill of Bussy, where he met Blucher. It is not necessary to go into the details of this interview. Suffice it to say that Wellington agreed with Blucher that he would come to the latter's assistance at Ligny, *if he was not himself attacked.*

At 11 A.M. Ney received from Napoleon a letter giving him detailed instructions as to the movements of the French army. The Emperor told Ney that he intended attacking the Prussians at Ligny, driving them back on Gembloux. Ney was then to march on Brussels, and Napoleon, marching by the Sombreffe-Quatre-Bras road with his Imperial Guard, would support him. Thus, according to the letter, Ney's movements were to wait upon Napoleon's. This interpretation was some cause of Ney's delays on the 16th.

Soon after the receipt of Napoleon's letter, Ney received an order from Soult, chief of the Staff, directing him to move the First and Second Corps, and Kellermann's Cavalry, on Quatre-Bras, drive back the enemy, and reconnoitre as far as he could towards Nivelles and Brussels; also to push a division to Genappe, and another towards Marbais, so as to open communication with Napoleon's left between Sombreffe and Quatre-Bras. Napoleon's intention was to reach Brussels by daybreak on the 17th, having defeated the Prussians, and Ney having defeated the English!

In accordance with this order, Ney sent instructions to Reille and d'Erlon. These were to the following effect:—The First, Second, and Third Divisions of d'Erlon's Corps were to move to Frasnes; the Fourth Division of that Corps, with Piré's Cavalry, was to move to Marbais; Kellermann's Cavalry Corps to Frasnes and Liberchies.

Just at this time, a message from Reille reached Ney, stating that Girard (not Gérard, who commanded the Fourth Corps) had sent in a report that strong columns of Prussians were moving along the Namur-Nivelles road, with heavy masses behind them. (These were Pirch's I. troops deploying at St Amand and Ligny.) Reille had seen Napoleon's letter to Ney, and read its contents, but he wrote to Ney that he would wait the latter's instructions, while he prepared his troops for instant march. Another order from Napoleon reached Ney at this moment. It stated that the Marshal was to unite the First and Second Corps with Kellermann's Cavalry, and drive the enemy from Quatre-Bras, thus distinctly emphasising the previous order. The Emperor, who thought that Ney would then have an ample force to crush any troops which could be in front of him, stated that Grouchy was about to move on Sombreffe.

Girard's report as to the Prussian columns on the Namur road made Ney doubly anxious for his position. He therefore again sent urgent orders to Reille and d'Erlon to hasten up. At 2 P.M., in the belief that d'Erlon must be close behind, he moved to the attack of the Anglo-Dutch position with three infantry divisions (Bachelu's, Foy's and Jerome's, of Reille's Corps) and Piré's Division of Light Cavalry, with 5 batteries—a strength of 18,000 men and 40 guns. Opposed to him were the 7,000 infantry and 16 guns of the Prince of Orange.

It is not proposed to give an account of the battle of Quatre-Bras. It has been shown what an opportunity Ney had lost by not attacking earlier, and what his reasons were for not doing so. Picton's Division and the Duke of Brunswick's Division arrived early in the afternoon, and Wellington took over the command. These reinforcements, to which were added towards the close of the day, Alten's Division, Cooke's Division, two more Brunswick battalions and a battery of Brunswick artillery, gave Wellington a superiority in numbers over Ney, who was only reinforced by Kellermann's Cavalry Corps during the battle. D'Erlon's Corps had, in the meantime, been wandering between Ligny and Frasnes.

In its results the battle of Quatre-Bras was of great importance to both sides. Although Ney had not obtained possession of Quatre-Bras, and had not defeated Wellington's troops, nor driven them back on Brussels, yet he had effectually prevented Wellington joining with Blucher's right. He had not been guilty of disobeying orders, and he himself did not feel confident of victory when he attacked on the afternoon of the 16th. On the other hand, Wellington had, by his masterly defence, completely frustrated Ney's object. He was now in full possession of Quatre-Bras; he had gained a brilliant victory, and his divisions were still coming up from behind. Should he receive news of a Prussian victory at Ligny, he was prepared to attack Ney next morning, and, if successful, to join Blucher's right wing and fall upon Napoleon's left. If the Prussians were defeated at Ligny, he was ready to fall back and take up a position where Blucher could join him, and together they would attack Napoleon's combined forces.

To turn to events upon the Prussian side, Blucher's decision to stand at Ligny was determined by several strategical considerations. Firstly, the position he chose communicated with Wellington's left by 6 miles of very good road, along which co-operation on either hand could be easily effected. Secondly, he guarded the communications with Aix-la-Chapelle and the Prussian States. Thirdly, if the Allies should be defeated both at Quatre-Bras and at Ligny, then two parallel lines of retreat, the one upon Mont St Jean towards Brussels, and the other upon Wavre towards Louvain, were available, which would render possible a junction near the forest of Soignies. Fourthly, if Napoleon had advanced against Wellington by way of Mons, the Prussians, by concentrating at Sombreffe, could have marched to the Duke's assistance, leaving Zieten to watch Charleroi and the neighbourhood. Fifthly, if Napoleon had advanced on Namur, the Third Corps (Thielemann's) could have retreated as did Zieten's, and allowed time and protection for the First, Second, and possibly the Fourth Corps, while Wellington moved to join the Prussian right.

The situation of the Allied armies was not exactly that of the Austrians and Sardinians in Italy in 1796-97; there was the possibility of striking at their point of junction and of beating each army separately, but the short and excellent line of communication between the points of concentration of Wellington's and Blucher's armies, namely, the Quatre-Bras-Sombreffe road, afforded each army such easy and rapid means of effecting a junction, although, in fact, it was not actually used as a means of co-operation, that there was a "moral" influence in it which went a long way towards defeating Napoleon's object. This may sound somewhat exaggerated; but what was it that made Ney uneasy for his own right flank on the 15th-16th, before he attacked? The report sent by Girard that Prussian columns were on that road. What was Napoleon's fear during the battle of Ligny? That Wellington would send a force from Quatre-Bras to join Blucher's right, along this road. What was the chief advantage in Wellington's position at Quatre-Bras? This road again, which afforded a means of joining the Prussians at Ligny, had the occasion arisen. And in what way was this road of use to Blucher at Sombreffe? He could co-operate with Wellington if Napoleon had attacked *via* Mons.

Blucher had decided to fight at Ligny, even though he had little hope of the arrival of Bulow's Corps in time to join the battle. For he believed that Napoleon's forces were not superior to his own in numbers; he had selected the position previously, and had had it surveyed carefully; he hoped that he would be able to hold his own either until Bulow arrived, or until night put an end to the fight. In the event of the Fourth Corps reaching the field in time to take part, the extra weight in numbers would decide in Blucher's favour, or else the Corps would attack Napoleon's right flank at a time when his troops would be most fatigued. Or again, if night came on, sufficient time would have been gained for Bulow's arrival to be made certain before daybreak next day, when a successful attack on the French might confidently be expected. In both cases, any pressure on Wellington would be relieved, so that the Anglo-Dutch Army might combine with Blucher to overwhelm the whole of Napoleon's forces. Thus Blucher reasoned.

To refuse a battle would have meant a retreat along his communications with the Rhine, and Blucher was most unwilling to abandon his chances of joining with Wellington.

The battle itself will not be described; but d'Erlon's wanderings towards the field and away from it again, and the influence of these aimless manœuvres on the struggle, may be discussed here.

At eight o'clock that morning (the 16th),

Napoleon had sent orders to Ney to detach one Division of his force to Marbais, so as to support the Emperor and attack in rear the Prussian right, while the battle of Ligny was at its height. At 2 P.M., he had ordered Ney to attack and defeat whatever force might be in front of him (he had ascertained that Ney must be greatly superior in numbers to the force that opposed him), and then to move along the Namur road and fall on Blucher's rear. At 3.15 P.M. this order was reiterated, and in the most emphatic manner was Ney ordered to bring the whole of his forces to bear on the Prussian right and rear. When, therefore, at 5.30 P.M., Napoleon was preparing his greatest blow at Blucher and getting in readiness his Reserves to crush the Prussian Centre at Ligny, the news that a strong column of infantry, cavalry, and artillery was making for Fleurus on the French left arrived, and it might have been guessed that this was a part of Ney's forces, acting in accordance with the instructions sent to the Marshal, but sadly in the wrong direction. Instead of moving against the Prussian right, this column was making for the left rear of the French. Vandamme, who forwarded the report to the Emperor, suspended his movements, and Girard fell back with his Division, until the uncertainty should be cleared up. For it *was* possible, perhaps, that Wellington had overcome Ney and was marching to assist Blucher; Ney had sent no tidings during the day. Napoleon, at first, believed that the force was the Division despatched by Ney in accordance with the eight o'clock order; but he reflected that the numbers were too great for a Division, and that Ney had been ordered to send the force by Marbais. Then, when Vandamme's suspicions were supported by a second report, he became extremely uneasy; he suspended his projected attack on the Prussian centre: and sent off an officer of his staff to ascertain the truth. At 7 P.M., nearly two hours after the first appearance of the strange column, the staff-officer returned, with the tidings that d'Erlon's whole Corps was at hand, and was marching to join Napoleon's left. On the receipt of this news, the advance of the Imperial Guard was renewed, and Girard's Division resumed its former position in line.

How d'Erlon had arrived in this position may be explained with little difficulty. When Napoleon's aide-de-camp, Laurent, reached Gosselies with the morning order, he found that the First Corps was already marching towards Quatre-Bras, and that d'Erlon himself had gone forward to Frasnes. Laurent hastened to find him, and on overtaking the columns of the First Corps on his way, he took upon himself the responsibility of changing their direction towards St Amand. D'Erlon, on learning what had been done, rode off at once to join his Corps, sending word to Ney to inform him what had happened. The road from Frasnes towards St Amand lay through Villers-Perruin, and it was this direction which brought the column into such an unexpected position towards the French rear. On reaching Villers-Perruin, however, d'Erlon sent out a Light Cavalry Brigade to his left, as a precautionary measure. This Brigade encountered a Prussian Brigade of Hussars and Lancers under Marwitz, who withdrew slowly and in good order. Girard's Division, perceiving the Prussians retire, became reassured, and moved forward to its original position. But now, d'Erlon received from Ney a most urgent and peremptory order to rejoin him at once. D'Erlon, who acted under Ney's immediate orders, decided that it was his duty to obey those orders; and since he had received no definite instructions from the Emperor as to how he should act when he had brought his Corps on the field, he turned about and left the ground. Thus he was too late in his return to be of use to Ney at Quatre-Bras, and the eccentric direction given to his columns, although the natural outcome of his previous dispositions, served to postpone Napoleon's great attack with his Guard for two hours; and, when the addition of 20,000 men might have entirely overwhelmed the Prussians, he calmly withdrew his men.

D'Erlon's error was his inaction when he arrived on the field, and not so much his diversion from Ney's orders. He must have known that he could not return to Quatre-Bras in time to be of any service; but that by following up Marwitz, and falling on the rear of the Prussian right wing, he would be most likely to render the very greatest assistance to Napoleon. How he could have failed to realise the importance of his presence at such a juncture surpasses all imagination. The very fact that Marwitz's Brigade had been able to present some show of compactness before Jacquinot's Cavalry might have proved to him that there was still a stout resistance to be expected on the part of the Prussians. Again, we think Napoleon should have sent instructions as to how d'Erlon should act, by his aide-de-camp, in the event of the strange column being French. Had d'Erlon remained on the left wing to assist Ney, Quatre-Bras might have been won by the French. Had he realised the uselessness of a return march to Ney when he was yet at hand to help Napoleon, and thrown all his weight into the struggle at Ligny, he would have been of the greatest use in overwhelming the Prussians.

Such mistakes as these are unexpected, and therefore happen, in war.

CHAPTER II

THE THIRD PRUSSIAN CORPS AND GROUCHY'S FORCES

THE Third Prussian Corps, commanded by Lieut.-General Thielemann, entered on the campaign of 1815 with a total strength of 23,980 men and 48 guns. There were four divisions[1] of infantry, containing from six to nine battalions each. These were composed as follows:—

NINTH DIVISION—Major-General BORCKE—

	Battns.	Men.
8th and 30th Regiments of the Line	3 }	6,752
1st KURMARK Landwehr Regiment	6 }	

TENTH DIVISION—Colonel KAMPFEN—

27th Regiment of the Line	3 }	4,045
2nd KURMARK Landwehr Regiment	3 }	

ELEVENTH DIVISION—Colonel LUCK—

3rd and 4th KURMARK Landwehr Regiments	6	3,634

TWELFTH DIVISION—Colonel STULPNAGEL—

31st Regiment of the Line	3 }	6,180
5th and 6th KURMARK Landwehr Regiments	6 }	

TOTAL Infantry, 30 battalions	20,611 men.

---

[1] The Prussians called them "brigades"—but as they varied in strength from 6 to 9 battalions (although the battalions were weak) I have substituted the word "divisions," as they corresponded to the infantry divisions in the French army.

The cavalry numbered 2,405 men, in two brigades, as follows:—

RESERVE CAVALRY—General HOBE.

Colonel MARWITZ's Brigade—

	Squadrons.	Men.
7th Uhlans	3	
8th Uhlans	4	925
9th Hussars	3	

Colonel Count LOTTUM's Brigade—

	Squadrons.	Men.
5th Uhlans	3	
7th Dragoons	5	
3rd KURMARK Landwehr	4	1,480
6th ,, ,,	4	

TOTAL Cavalry, 26 squadrons or 2,405 men.

The Reserve Artillery of the Corps, under Colonel Mohnhaupt, numbered 964 men, with 48 guns. The guns were divided up into one 12 pr. foot battery (No. 7), two 6 pr. foot batteries (Nos. 18 and 35), and three batteries of horse artillery (Nos. 18, 19 and 20). Each battery, horse and foot, had 8 guns.

SUMMARY.

Infantry	20,611 men.	
Cavalry	2,405 ,,	
Artillery	964 ,,	48 guns.
TOTAL	23,980 ,,	

As regards organisation, the Corps was an early form of the modern Army Corps, although there were no "divisional" troops attached to the infantry divisions, and the "corps" troops consisted of the cavalry and artillery brought together as "reserves" under separate commanders, and the necessary engineers and train. It is curious to note that, in the actual fighting, the artillery and cavalry, more especially the former, were divided up, as soon as the battle began. The idea which prevailed in those days, of cavalry "reserves" and cavalry corps, composed of two or more "divisions," is a marked feature of the later Napoleonic era; and the fact that both disappeared after 1815 goes some way to proving the futility, or, rather, the disadvantages of such organisations, as Napoleon meant them. No larger bodies of cavalry than divisions have been used since; nor has any army since gone forth with a cavalry "reserve."

The Prussian infantry regiment had three battalions, one of which was the Fusilier battalion. The battalions averaged from 750 to 600 men each; the divisions, from six to nine battalions. The cavalry regiment was composed of from three to five squadrons; the brigade, of from three to four regiments. The batteries of artillery, horse and foot, consisted of 8 guns each, and the personnel of the battery numbered 160 on the average. Thielemann's Corps was weak in cavalry and artillery, as measured by modern notions; the proportions were 1 cavalryman to nearly every 10 infantry, and 2·4 guns per 1,000 infantry.

The spirit of the troops was excellent, and they were led by brave and capable officers. The old hatred of the French still burned in the hearts of the Prussian soldiers, and they desired nothing so much as to be given an opportunity of revenging Jena and Auerstadt. Their officers were well trained and full of enthusiasm; they had confidence in their men, and the latter had confidence in them.

At Ligny, the Corps won praise for its firm behaviour, and although, during the battle, it had not been hard pressed at any time, at the close of the day, when the Prussian right and centre were broken, it maintained its original position before Sombreffe and on Blucher's left, enabling the First and Second Corps to withdraw from the field in safety. When it was almost too dark to distinguish friend from foe, Thielemann made a bold counter-stroke with two of his battalions. Major Dittfurth, with the First and Second Battalions of the 30th Prussian Regiment, moved out from Mont Potriaux, which village he had held throughout the afternoon, crossed the Ligny, and made a demonstration against Grouchy on the French right, in order to hinder the pursuit of the broken Prussian centre. A regiment of Dragoons from Excelmans' Corps charged the Second Battalion, but was repulsed, and Dittfurth, gaining courage, pushed his men further and seized a hill occupied in force by the French. Two more cavalry charges were launched against them, but were also repulsed. And now a division of Lobau's Corps, in a heavy column, advanced against the First Battalion; but Dittfurth, with great skill and presence of mind, so disposed the Second Battalion as to bring a heavy flanking fire on the French, who suffered severe losses from this fire, and who, being uncertain in the darkness of the strength of the enemy, withdrew. Dittfurth now checked his advance, having successfully prevented the French from pressing too hard on the Prussian centre, and withdrew his battalions to Mont Potriaux. A French cavalry brigade charged up to the barrier on the Fleurus high-road to gain Sombreffe, but the Prussians of the Ninth Division beat them off.

When the battle died out in the darkness, Thielemann held the line Sombreffe-Point du Jour. He remained in position until 3 A.M. on the 17th, when the whole field had been evacuated by the First and Second Corps; and then he commenced, in perfect order, his retreat to Gembloux, where he was to join the Fourth

Corps, under Bulow, who had arrived there during the night.

Thielemann's men were not discouraged by the loss of the battle of Ligny; on the contrary, they were full of spirit and determination; their behaviour under fire had been excellent, and they eagerly waited for a further opportunity of trying their strength with their formidable enemies.

The losses in the corps at Ligny amounted to about 1,000 men killed and wounded, and 7 guns lost.

The force detached by Napoleon for the pursuit of the Prussians, and given over to Marshal Grouchy, numbered 33,611 men and 96 guns. It was composed as follows:—

THIRD CORPS—Vandamme.

    Eighth Division—(Lefol)

	Battns.	Men.
15th Light Infantry, 23rd, 37th, and 64th Regiments of the Line	11	
Tenth Division—(Habert) 22nd, 34th, 70th and 88th Regiments of the Line	12	14,508
Eleventh Division—(Berthézène) 12th, 33rd, 56th, and 86th Regiments of the Line	8	
Battalions Infantry	31	

Artillery

	Men.	Guns.
4 batteries Foot[1] Artillery (8 guns each)	782	32
Engineers	146	

TOTALS, THIRD CORPS

Infantry	14,508
Artillery	782, 32 guns.
Engineers	146
	15,536 men.

FOURTH CORPS—Gérard.

Twelfth Division—(Pecheux)

    30th, 63rd, and 96th Regiments of the Line . . . . .   Battns. 10 ⎫

Thirteenth Division—(Vichery)

    48th, 59th, 69th, and 76th Regiments of the Line . . . 8 ⎬ Men. 12,589

Fourteenth Division—(Hulot)

    9th Light Infantry, 44th, 50th, and 111th Regiments of the Line . 8 ⎭

                  Battalions Infantry . . 26

Seventh Cavalry Division—(Maurin)   Squadrons. Men.

    6th Hussars . . . . . 3 ⎫
    8th Chasseurs . . . . 3 ⎬ 758

Reserve Cavalry Division—(Jacquinot)

    6th, 11th, 15th, and 16th Dragoons   16   1,608

Artillery   Guns.

    4 Batteries Foot Artillery . . 32 ⎫
    1 Battery Horse Artillery . . 6 ⎬ 1,538

Engineers 201

---

[1] The French foot batteries contained 8 guns; the horse batteries, 6 guns. The horse battery belonging to Vandamme's Corps had been detached with Domon's Light Cavalry Division, to the Left Wing.

TOTALS, FOURTH CORPS

Infantry	12,589 men.
Cavalry	2,366 ,,
Artillery	1,538 ,,
Engineers	201 ,,
Total	**16,694** ,, 38 guns

TWENTY-FIRST DIVISION — Teste. Detached from Lobau's Corps.

	Battns.	Men.
8th Light Infantry, 40th, 65th, and 75th Regiments of the Line	5	2,316

Artillery attached to the Division—	Guns.	
1 Battery Foot Artillery	8	161

Total, Teste's Division . 2,477 men, 8 guns.

Cavalry

FOURTH CAVALRY DIVISION (belonging to 1st Cavalry Corps) under Pajol (commanding First Cavalry Corps)—

	Squadrons.	Men.
1st, 4th, and 5th Hussars	12	1,234

Artillery attached to this Cavalry Division—	Guns.	Men.
1 Battery Horse Artillery	6	154

SECOND CAVALRY CORPS (Excelmans')—

Ninth Cavalry Division—(Strolz) Squadrons.
5th, 13th, 15th, and 20th Dragoons 16 ⎫
Tenth Cavalry Division (Chastel) ⎬ 2,817
4th, 12th, 14th, and 17th Dragoons 15 ⎭

Artillery attached to the Second Cavalry Corps—

	Guns.	
2 Batteries Horse Artillery	12	246

SUMMARY OF GROUCHY'S FORCES.

	Infantry.	Cavalry.	Artillery.	Engrs.	Guns.
Third Corps, Vandamme	14,508	—	782	146	32
Fourth Corps, Gérard	12,589	2,366	1,538	201	38
Twenty-First Division, Teste	2,316	—	161	—	8
Fourth Cav. Division, Pajol	—	1,234	154	—	6
Second Cav. Corps, Excelmans'	—	2,817	246	—	12
	29,413	6,417	2,881	347	96
Deducting losses at Ligny	3,940	907	600	—	—
TOTALS	25,473	5,510	2,281	347	96

33,611 men, 96 guns.

It will be seen that Grouchy was given a large proportion of cavalry, although the numbers composing the different units were in most cases very short. Thus the Second Cavalry Corps numbered only 2,817 men, whereas a modern cavalry corps, or rather, two cavalry divisions (as no modern army organises larger bodies of cavalry than divisions), would amount to 9,000 or 10,000 men. The Fourth Cavalry Division (commanded by Soult, brother of the Chief of the Staff, although under the immediate orders of Pajol, commanding the First Cavalry Corps), numbered 1,234 instead of 4,896 men, as the modern British Cavalry Division at war strength would number. The horse batteries consisted of 6 guns, as opposed to 8 in the Prussian horse batteries. The foot batteries contained 8 guns each on both sides. The infantry battalions were weak, averaging from 400 to 500 men. Only Gérard's Corps was well supplied with cavalry; the remainder of the cavalry was formed in divisions or corps. The idea of cavalry reserves served its purpose on the field of battle in the earlier Napoleonic days, but for such operations as Grouchy was about to carry out, the organisations were too cumbersome.

Grouchy's men were good soldiers, but without discipline, without confidence in their leaders. This would seem paradoxical; but as far as courage, determination, and tenacity make good soldiers, they were excellent. Houssaye said of Napoleon's last army: "He had never before handled an instrument of war, which was at once so formidable and so fragile." Indeed, Ligny proved well enough the impetuosity and dash of the French soldiers, but it was only the influence of victory which impelled them; had they suffered defeat, they would, not improbably, have been panic-stricken. They worshipped the Emperor as their idol, but for their more immediate superiors they had little respect. De Bourmont's desertion on the 15th June, as the army crossed the frontier, had an injurious effect on the men's feelings; murmurs rose from the ranks, and mistrust of their generals was everywhere visible. The Republican spirit was in them, but now it needed even more than the personal force of the Emperor to set it blazing again.

At Ligny, the Third (Vandamme's) and the Fourth (Gérard's) Corps had borne the brunt of the fighting, and had splendidly attacked the stout-hearted Prussians posted in the villages and on the banks of the stream. The final success of their onslaught against Blucher's centre and right, where the terrible slaughter gave evidence of the stubbornness of the fight, speaks well for the quality of the men. The cavalry had done little except execute some occasional charges against Thielemann's Divisions, and seize Tongrenelles and Balâtre: although Milhaud's Cuirassiers (with whom we are not concerned in this narrative) broke through the centre at Ligny at the close of the day.

The losses were heavy in Vandamme's and Gérard's Corps, especially among the infantry—nearly 4000 killed and wounded; while the cavalry lost 900 and the artillery 600.

There was very little of the spirit of co-operation between Napoleon's generals in this campaign. They all had petty jealousies, but none so strongly as Vandamme, Gérard and Grouchy. And these were the men to whom the pursuit of the Prussians had been entrusted!

Grouchy was, and had been, a brilliant leader

of cavalry. He had not the impetuous dash of Murat, the greatest of Napoleon's cavalry commanders, but he had mastered the art of handling large masses of horsemen. He was a soldier of twenty years' war experience, and he had distinguished himself at Hohenlinden, Friedland, Eylau, Wagram, and in Russia. He was given the command of the four corps of reserve cavalry—Pajol's, Milhaud's, Excelmans', and Kellermann's—early in June 1815, but after Ligny he was appointed to a higher and more responsible post—commander of the Right Wing, charged with the duty of following up the Prussians and preventing them from joining Wellington.

Grouchy was not a fit man for independent command. In spite of his exploits in former days, he had never before been exercised in so great a responsibility. And no sooner had he received the appointment than he began expostulating and raising objections. Yet whom else could Napoleon choose? Murat was no longer with him. Davoût was Minister of War and Commandant of Paris—he could not be spared. These were the two men who should have been in Ney's place and Grouchy's. Lannes, Dessaix, or Masséna would have well filled the post instead of Grouchy, but Lannes and Dessaix were dead, and Masséna's services were not available.

Napoleon was not now served by his lieutenants as he had been of old, and his generals were not of the stuff which had composed his earlier subordinates. The truth is that he could no longer ignore the claims of rank and seniority. In former days, he could promote to the highest ranks those whom he chose, and those "who had yet a name to make."

Of the generals in the Waterloo campaign, on the French side, who could have taken Grouchy's place? We cannot say that Gérard could, simply because he advised Grouchy at Walhain to do the right thing! He was junior, too, to Vandamme. And Vandamme was a rough, uncouth soldier. He had commanded a division at the age of twenty-seven, and had exhibited great qualities as a fighter, but for so important a command as Grouchy's, he was not the man. Had he been a really capable general, would he not have risen beyond one step in rank since 1799? He was a divisional commander in 1799, and a corps commander in 1815; for sixteen years he had not risen. Besides, he quarrelled both with Gérard and Grouchy (as well as with Soult), and his slow movements on the 15th June, as Napoleon crossed the Sambre, were not entirely due to ignorance of orders.

Soult was the only possible alternative, but

he was already Chief of the Staff. As Chief of the Staff he was a failure, but he could not be replaced, and Napoleon desired to have a Marshal of France by his side. Soult was in disgrace on Napoleon's return from Elba, but the Emperor pardoned him and appointed him to the post that should have been given to Davoût, once the latter had put the organization of the armies in fair order. Suchet was a better man than Soult for Chief of the Staff, and Soult was a better man than Grouchy for the command of the right wing. But Suchet already commanded the army of the Alps.

However, at the time, it was not possible for Napoleon to make an alternative selection, and Grouchy was the only man available. Up to this point there had been no reason to doubt his capabilities, and it is not fair to criticise the man until his faults have been clearly proved; it must be remembered that mistakes in war are inevitable; and the "general who makes no mistakes in war has not waged war for long."[1]

[1] Turenne.

CHAPTER III

THE RETREAT OF THIELEMANN'S CORPS FROM SOMBREFFE

GENERAL GNEISENAU, who had taken Blucher's place in command during his temporary disablement (his horse had rolled on him during a close pursuit by French cavalry), gave orders at the close of the battle of Ligny for the First and Second Corps (Zieten's and Pirch I.'s) to retreat upon Tilly, and for Thielemann to cover the withdrawal until the centre and right were clear of the field. He was then to retire upon Tilly, or, should he not be able to make for that point, to retreat upon Gembloux, and unite there with the Fourth Corps under Bulow. Thielemann and Bulow were then to effect their junction with the main army.

The First and Second Corps spent the night of the 16th between Mellery, Tilly and Gentinnes, on the two roads which lead towards Wavre, and join at Mont St Guibert. Thielemann remained upon the field of battle until 3 A.M., when he began his retreat upon Gembloux. It was only after the First and Second Corps had reached Tilly and Gentinnes in the middle of the night that Wavre was chosen as the rallying point. It is most probable that Gneisenau's immediate object was to move the shattered Corps clear of the battlefield under the firm protection of Thielemann's men, before he cast about for a point of assembly. To ensure an orderly retreat and the soonest possible revival of the defeated troops was the first thing to be aimed at. And Gneisenau, who is credited with initiating the brilliant strategy of the retreat to Wavre, took care first of all to rally his men; for he must have feared a vigorous pursuit by the French, who, he supposed, would soon force Thielemann to withdraw.

The retreat of a defeated army in face of the enemy is one of the most difficult and delicate operations in war. The two chief causes of the success of the Prussian retreat from Ligny were the favourable darkness and Thielemann's firm behaviour at Sombreffe.

It is not necessary to enter here into the details of the retreat of Zieten and Pirch I., except in so far as they bear upon the subject of Thielemann's withdrawal, but a brief description of their movements may be given. The two Corps retreated by the roads Tilly-Mont St

Guibert and Gentinnes - Mont St Guibert. Pirch's Corps, arriving second, remained at Mont St Guibert for a time as rear-guard, to protect the cross-roads, and still further to steady the men; for the best troops are unsteadied by retreat. Zieten pushed on to Wavre, arriving at noon, and took his troops across the Dyle, halting at Bierges, about a mile south-west of the town. Pirch followed, but did not cross the Dyle; he halted between Aisemont and St Anne, two villages a mile and two miles south-east of Wavre.

Gneisenau had given Thielemann the choice of retreating upon Tilly or Gembloux, a point which could only be decided according to circumstances. Both of these places were on roads converging upon Wavre, and at Gembloux there were no less than four alternative routes. When Thielemann made preparations for his retreat, he considered carefully the respective advantages of these two points. If he chose Tilly, he would have to make a flank march along the Namur road to Marbais and strike northwards from there. He would then be following the road taken by Pirch I. and Zieten; but this very fact was an objection, because there were sure to be disabled waggons, broken-down guns, and hundreds of stragglers to hinder his passage. He could only use one road, too. But was it safe to expose himself to an attack on his flank by the French, while he was marching on Marbais? Certainly not; for he could not possibly slip by in the darkness; it would be daylight before his rear had cleared Sombreffe. He turned to Gembloux. The road from Sombreffe to that village was direct. He would not expose either flank by marching along that road. It was not encumbered with the remnants of a retreating force; and his troops were already in an easy position to withdraw. At Gembloux, he might expect to meet Bulow's Corps; and if so, the two could unite and use any of the four roads from thence towards Wavre. It would save a great deal of time if he could employ more than one road for his march, but he would have to make ample provision for guarding the rear of his columns, and it would be more difficult to protect three columns than one. He expected to be closely pursued the moment he began to retreat, but he would leave a strong rear-guard to cover him.

But it must be remembered that Thielemann, at this time, did not know whither the retreat was ordered, beyond Gembloux. He guessed that it was in the direction of Wavre on account of the route taken by the First and Second Corps.

He therefore decided to retire upon Gembloux. During the night, he drew in all his outposts, and collected his somewhat scattered battalions. In the battle, battalions from one division had become mingled with battalions from another, and the Reserve Cavalry Division now consisted only of Lottum's Brigade; Marwitz's Brigade had retired with Zieten by Gentinnes. General Borcke, with the Ninth Division, and General Hobe with Lottum's Cavalry Brigade, were left as rear-guard, drawn up along the Namur road, between Sombreffe and Point du Jour. At 2 A.M. the head of the Corps, consisting of the Reserve Artillery, moved off, and by 4 A.M., after sunrise, the rear-guard started. Two hours' marching brought the main body to Gembloux. Here Thielemann, having found out that Bulow with the Fourth Corps had reached Baudeset, on the old Roman road, about 3 miles behind Gembloux, called a halt to rest his troops. It was a hazardous step, so far as he knew, for the French might be upon him at any moment; but it must be remembered that he had had no further instructions as to his future movements, beyond the bare fact that he was to join Bulow and together they were to unite with the main army. But where were the First and Second Corps?

Thielemann sent word to Bulow to ask him if he had had any instructions as to their movements, and telling him that he had not yet been followed by the French. Bulow could give no information; but at 9.30 A.M., an aide-de-camp from Blucher arrived with orders for the Fourth Corps to march on Dion-le-Mont, a village 3 miles east of Wavre, *viâ* Walhain' and Corbaix. The orders further stated that Bulow was to post his rear-guard (the Fourteenth Division, under Ryssel—9 battalions, or 6,953 infantry) at Vieux Sart at the end of the march, so as to give notice of the approach of the French; and to send a force consisting of 1 cavalry regiment, 2 battalions of infantry, and 2 guns of horse artillery, to Mont St Guibert, to support Colonel Sohr, who was at Tilly with a cavalry brigade and 4 guns acting as rear-guard to the First and Second Corps. When Sohr fell back, the detachment from Bulow's Corps was to remain at Mont St Guibert as rear-guard on the Tilly road. Bulow therefore detached Colonel Ledebur with the 10th Hussars, the Fusilier battalions of the 11th regiment of the line and the 1st Pomeranian Landwehr, and 2 guns of No. 12 Battery Horse Artillery, to Mont St Guibert, while the remainder of his Corps marched upon Dion-le-Mont. The movement was painfully slow, and not until 10.30 P.M. were the troops in position.

Thielemann, meanwhile, who had received orders to continue his march on Wavre, made preparations to resume his road. At 2 P.M., his troops having gained a sound and well-earned rest, secure, strange to say, from pursuit — for not a Frenchman had been seen — he again advanced, and passed by Ernage, Nil Perrieux, Corbaix, and La Baraque. He reached Wavre with his main body at 8 P.M., having covered the 15 miles in six hours, and passed through to La Bavette, a mile north of Wavre, where he halted for the night. His rear-guard (the Ninth Division and Lottum's Cavalry Brigade) did not reach the Dyle until midnight; they bivouacked on the right bank. Marwitz, with his Cavalry Brigade, which had retired by Gentinnes with Zieten, now rejoined the Third Corps, and the troops which had been detached two days before to Dinant (a battalion of the 3rd Kurmark Landwehr, belonging to the Eleventh Division, and two squadrons of the 6th Kurmark Landwehr Cavalry, belonging to Lottum's Brigade) also arrived. Thus the retreat of the Third Corps was accomplished in security, and accompanied by none of the disastrous effects of a defeat.

Defeat at the hands of so great a master of war as Napoleon usually meant annihilation. To follow up his victory, to pursue the retreating force, and to leave no vestige of fighting power in the vanquished, is the aim and object of every general who wins a battle. When the Prussians were defeated at Ligny, the advantage of vigorous pursuit with all the available cavalry and Lobau's Corps would have been enormous. The whole aim of Napoleon's strategy had been to crush the Prussians, and to prevent them from interfering with his attack on Wellington. He had found Blucher ready to fight at Ligny, and he had beaten him. To allow Blucher to retreat with fighting power left in his army was the very result to be avoided at all cost. Then why did not Napoleon follow up his victory? What are the facts?

The battle was over at about 9 P.M., on the 16th, the broken centre of Blucher's line retreating by Bry. Darkness covered the field. Vandamme's Third Corps, Gérard's Fourth Corps, and Milhaud's Cuirassiers had well-nigh exhausted themselves in their vigorous attacks, but Excelmans, Pajol, with their two Cavalry Corps, and Lobau with the Sixth Corps, were available for the pursuit. Their troops were comparatively fresh; Lobau had only arrived on the field towards the end of the day. But no attempt was made to hinder the retreat of Zieten and Pirch I. Thielemann maintained a firm hold on Sombreffe, but he did not cover Bry or the roads to Tilly.

The French bivouacked on the battlefield; the Third Corps in front of St Amand; the Fourth Corps in front of Ligny; the Imperial Guard on the hill at Bry; the Cavalry behind Sombreffe (and facing Thielemann); and the Sixth Corps behind Ligny. Grouchy's vedettes were almost within ear-shot of Thielemann's outposts. Yet, although Thielemann's rear-guard did not begin to retreat until after sunrise, nothing was discovered, and when day broke the French were still slumbering heavily in their bivouacs. Their vedettes should have been moved forward with the first streak of dawn, to feel for the Prussians. They should, at least, have *heard* something, even if they saw nothing; for a retreat cannot be carried out with absolute silence. There must be cracking of whips, rumbling of wheels, cries from the drivers, and excitement among the animals, however quiet the troops themselves may be. If even half-a-dozen patrols had been sent out to gather information as soon as day broke, the French could not have failed to discover Thielemann's retreat, and, having found it, they would not have had much difficulty in locating its direction. There seemed to be a fixed resolve to let the Prussians go free.

On the other hand, there were many reasons which caused Napoleon's decision not to pursue during that night. The Prussian right wing had not been crushed; it retreated because its position was dangerous as soon as the centre gave way. The left wing, Thielemann's Corps, was very firm. There was also the probable arrival of Bulow's Corps by the Namur road. The Prussian army was still full of fight. No news from Ney had been received during the day. Napoleon was in entire ignorance as to the state of affairs on his left wing. Lastly, a pursuit by night, especially the pursuit of a still formidable enemy, is a most dangerous task.

But if there was no actual pursuit by night, means should have been taken to ascertain the direction of the retreat, for it was all-important to discover this, and a very few patrols would have sufficed to gather the information.

If there were good and sufficient reasons for not pursuing by night, there were none for the delay when day broke. Grouchy had been summoned to Napoleon's headquarters at Fleurus at eleven o'clock at night, when he received orders to send the two Corps of cavalry under Pajol and Excelmans to pursue the enemy at daybreak. Grouchy then remained at Fleurus until 9 A.M., when he was ordered to accompany Napoleon on a tour of inspection of the battlefield! What was the object of visiting the field at this critical time? This behaviour was most unusual on Napoleon's part. Was he affected at the sight of so much bloodshed, and desirous of cheering the injured? He had witnessed too much slaughter on the battlefield to be touched with emotion, which can only be a weakness in a general. The general should fight with as little loss of human life as possible, but he should not be filled with pitiful reflections in the crisis of a campaign. Besides, the wounded, both French and Prussians, were being cared for. There seems to have been some physical cause for Napoleon's strange behaviour on the morning of the 17th; for after he had visited the field he discussed politics and affairs in Paris with his generals! He wasted the hours until 11 A.M. Shortly before that hour he had received news from Ney as to the battle at Quatre-Bras, and this decided him to make his final arrangements. He ordered Lobau to take the Sixth Corps (less Teste's Division) to Marbais, to support Ney and attack Wellington's left flank. He himself would follow with the Imperial Guard and Domon's Light Cavalry Division. Grouchy was to take the Third and Fourth Corps, Teste's Division, and Pajol's and Excelmans' Cavalry, and pursue the Prussians. Thus only at 11 A.M. on the morning of the 17th did Napoleon give his orders for the pursuit.

Of course, it was necessary to know what had happened at Quatre-Bras, but the fact of having received no news from Ney, and, besides, no assistance from that quarter during the battle at Ligny, should have suggested to Napoleon that Ney must certainly be in difficulties. Had he been victorious at Quatre-Bras, he would have been certain to send a message of some kind, even if he sent no reinforcements to St Amand. Ney, under the circumstances, would have been much more likely to send news if he had been successful, than during a time when all his attention was occupied with the fighting around him.

But this does not explain why Napoleon neglected to follow up the Prussians. As soon as day broke, there were two most important steps to take. Firstly, to find out where the Prussians had gone to, since touch with them had been lost during the night, and to drive them away from Wellington; and secondly, to find out how Ney had fared, and to send him help if he needed it.

Now, a force in retreat does not require an equivalent force to pursue it. The moral advantages with the victor enable him to press vigorously with fewer troops. So the force detached under Grouchy (33,600 men) was ample to follow up the Prussians, and to beat even the fresh Corps (Bulow's) which Napoleon suspected in the vicinity of Gembloux. True, Grouchy's force was required to do something more than follow up and beat Thielemann's Corps, or Thielemann's and Bulow's combined: but what could be Napoleon's object in keeping back any troops at Ligny? Having detailed Grouchy's force, the remaining troops might have been pushed to Quatre-Bras at dawn, and *not* at midday.

Whatever may be said in extenuation of Napoleon's delay and inactivity on the morning of the 17th, the actual circumstances of the case did not warrant his wasting his time on the previous day's battlefield and discussing politics with his generals when all his energies should have been concentrated on the great crisis at hand; and having so far successfully carried out his brilliant strategic plan, he should most certainly have followed up his success and made sure that he *had* separated Blucher from Wellington.

It is easy to criticise Napoleon now, when the results of his inactivity are so apparent, but by taking into account the actual circumstances at the time, as they must have presented themselves to him, without reference to the results, and by putting ourselves in the position of the man in command, it is impossible to find sufficient reasons for his delays.

What actually happened in the pursuit of the Prussians will be related in the next chapter.

CHAPTER IV

GROUCHY'S PURSUIT OF THE PRUSSIANS

GROUCHY had received orders from Napoleon at about 11 P.M. on the night of the 16th to send the two cavalry corps of Pajol and Excelmans at daybreak in pursuit of the Prussians. He was not told in which direction to pursue, or whether to pursue Thielemann only.

Accordingly, when Pajol started off at 4 A.M., there were no signs to show in which direction Thielemann had retired. Taking Soult's Division of Light Cavalry, Pajol started off from Balâtre and made his way across to the Namur road, under the impression that this was the true line of retreat. He sent in a despatch from Balâtre (he must have written it very soon after his troops had started) to the Emperor, stating that he was "pursuing the enemy, who were in full retreat towards Liège and Namur," and that he had already made many prisoners. Shortly after striking the Namur road, he came upon a Prussian Horse Battery (No. 14) which had "withdrawn during the battle of Ligny to replenish its ammunition waggons" (!) but had failed to fall in with the ammunition column. Thielemann had ordered it to retire on Gembloux, when he beat his retreat, but this it failed to do, and wandered about aimlessly near the Namur road. When Pajol's men came up, they captured the whole battery, in front of Le Mazy; and Pajol reported it in great glee to the Emperor. This tended to increase the belief that the Prussians were making for Namur. But Pajol, advancing some three miles beyond Le Mazy, without coming across further traces of the enemy, began at last to suspect that he was leading a wild goose chase. Accordingly he halted at Le Boquet, and sent out reconnoitring parties. At midday (while Thielemann was resting at Gembloux) he started off northwards on Saint-Denis, with the object of taking the road to Louvain. At Saint-Denis he was joined by Teste's Division, which had been sent to him by Napoleon. Thus Pajol was very far from being of use in the chase.

Meanwhile, Excelmans fared little better. Berton's Brigade of Dragoons, belonging to Excelmans' Corps, started off to follow Thielemann's rear-guard, whose departure was only noticed as it left Sombreffe. But Berton followed down the Namur road behind Pajol.

What was the advantage in searching the country which had just been passed by the First Cavalry Corps? It is hard to suppose that it was not known which way Pajol had taken. Berton got as far as Le Mazy, where he was told by some peasants that the Prussians had retreated by Gembloux. He therefore halted, sent back the news to Excelmans, and awaited instructions. It was unfortunate for the French that he did not think of sending this news *forward* to Pajol!

Instructions soon arrived, and Berton was ordered to march on Gembloux. He therefore marched up the valley of the Orneau, a small stream running southwards to the Sambre, and arrived in front of Gembloux at 9 A.M. Here he found the Prussian outposts, and descried, on the far side of the village, the whole of Thielemann's Corps taking their rest. Excelmans, with his remaining three brigades of cavalry, arrived before Gembloux, half an hour later, *i.e.* at 9.30 A.M. He saw that there were some 20,000 Prussians resting beyond the village, and yet he neglected to send back word to Grouchy immediately. He did not even inform Pajol of his discovery, so the latter was still wandering. Although he had 3,000 cavalry and 12 guns, Excelmans made no attempt to harass the Prussians, who, since they were resting, were obviously not ready to fight again. But his mistake lay not so much in his avoiding conflict as in his omission to send immediate news to Grouchy and Pajol. There can never be a mistake in sending back too much information to head-quarters (as far as the means of transmission allow); what is not required can there be disposed of.

So much for the efforts of Excelmans and Pajol to follow up the Prussians.

Grouchy, meanwhile, at 11.30 A.M., received the following written order from Napoleon:—

"Repair to Gembloux with the Cavalry Corps of Pajol and Excelmans, the Light Cavalry of the Fourth Corps, Teste's Division, and the Third and Fourth Corps of Infantry. You will send out scouts in the direction of Namur and Maestricht, and you will pursue the enemy. Reconnoitre his march, and tell me of his movements, that I may penetrate his designs. I shall move my head-quarters to Quatre-Bras, where the English still were this morning; our communication will then be direct by the Namur road. Should the enemy have evacuated Namur, write to the general in command of the Second Military Division at Charlemont, to occupy this town with a few battalions of National Guards. It is important to discover what Wellington and Blucher mean to do, and whether they meditate uniting their armies to cover Brussels and Liège by risking the fate of a battle. At all events, keep your two Infantry Corps continually together, within a mile of each other, reserving several ways of retreat;

place detachments of cavalry between, so as to be able to communicate with Head-quarters."

This order contains certain very definite instructions. First, Grouchy was to concentrate all his forces at Gembloux. Secondly, he was to reconnoitre towards Namur and Maestricht, as it was very possible (according to Napoleon's information) that the enemy had gone in those directions. Thirdly, he was to follow the tracks of the Prussians, and to try to discover what they intended to do.

As to the first, Grouchy was unaware that Excelmans, with his whole Corps, was already at Gembloux. But Pajol's report from Le Mazy might have helped him to come to the conclusion that the Prussians had not taken that direction.

Grouchy, when he had received his verbal instructions from Napoleon, had expostulated and expressed the opinion that no advantage would be obtained if he carried out the operations he was ordered to. He argued that the Prussians had already had twelve hours' start; that although no definite news had yet been received from the cavalry scouts, it was extremely likely that Blucher had retired on his base, Namur; and that in following the Prussians in this direction he would be moving further and further from Napoleon. He asked to be allowed to march to Quatre-Bras with the Emperor. But Napoleon, naturally enough, declined, and firmly repeated his orders to Grouchy, saying that it was his (Grouchy's) duty to find which route the Prussians had taken, and to attack them as soon as he found them.

Grouchy withdrew and proceeded to carry out his orders. But if he was so far convinced of the importance and infallibility of his own conclusions as to discuss them boldly before the Emperor, he certainly could not have been very hopeful or determined when he proceeded to carry out the very instructions against which he had been arguing!

He then sent orders to Vandamme, who was at St Amand, to march at once with the Third Corps to Point-du-Jour, at the junction of the Gembloux and Namur roads. He sent an aide-de-camp towards Gembloux to obtain news from Excelmans. (Not often is it necessary for a general to send one of his own Staff to gather news from the advanced cavalry!) He then went himself to Ligny to give Gérard his orders.

In starting Vandamme before Gérard, Grouchy made a serious mistake; for Gérard had over an hour to wait before he could march his troops off, since both Corps had to use the same road, and Vandamme was behind Gérard at the time. Vandamme's Corps had suffered less than Gérard's at Ligny the day before, but it was no longer a case of fearing an inferiority in numbers. Vandamme marched with incredible slowness. His advanced guard did not reach Point-du-Jour until 3 P.M.; (Thielemann was by this time an hour's march beyond Gembloux!) The roads were in a very bad state, it is true, and the heavy rain that was falling made marching difficult; also the passage of the Prussians had made the roads worse; but Point-du-Jour is less than 4 miles from St Amand.

Grouchy himself went to Point-du-Jour, arriving at the same time as Vandamme's advanced guard. Here he received his aide-de-camp, who had returned with news from Excelmans; who reported that "he was observing the enemy's army," and "would follow the Prussians as soon as ever they should begin to march" (Houssaye). Grouchy, instead of giving Vandamme and Gérard orders to hasten their march on Gembloux, and galloping there himself, made no effort to hurry. He accompanied Vandamme's Corps, which still continued with extraordinary slowness; and arrived at Gembloux at seven o'clock in the evening; taking four hours to cover 5 miles. Gérard arrived there two hours later. Thus at the end of the day, Grouchy's main body was less than 7 miles from Ligny; and he was supposed to be vigorously pressing the Prussians! He had not yet found the direction of their retreat! Compare, allowing even for the rain and the state of the roads, his rate of marching with Thielemann's, over the same road, a few hours previously; and compare Grouchy's subsequent retreat.

Napoleon's first instruction to Grouchy was to concentrate all his forces at Gembloux. To enable both Corps to arrive at Gembloux together, Gérard's should have marched off first and taken the cross-country road from Sombreffe to the old Roman road, and thence along to Gembloux. Vandamme would then have had a clear road past Point-du-Jour, undisturbed by Gérard's troops. As it was, Gérard's men had to traverse a road already cut up by the Prussians and Vandamme's Corps.

Excelmans had lost every opportunity. He should not have contented himself with watching the enemy; he should have made "feints," to cause the Prussians to disclose their intentions, or he should at least have discovered the direction of their movements. If he was too weak to attack even the rear-guard, he should have endeavoured to work round Thielemann and occupy him while Grouchy with the main body arrived. He should also have sent across to Pajol and asked him to work in towards his left so as still further to hamper Thielemann. But none of these things were done, and the Prussians were allowed to move off quietly, Excelmans merely following behind!

Even when Thielemann moved out of Gembloux at 2 P.M., it was three o'clock before Excelmans entered the village, and yet his scouts had been watching the Prussians since 9 A.M. He was content to march leisurely on to Sauvenière, a village 3 miles north of Gembloux.

Grouchy decided to halt at Gembloux for the night. Although there were still two hours of daylight left when Vandamme's Corps reached the village, yet it was ordered to bivouac there. Grouchy afterwards stated that the roads were too bad to march on, and the rain too heavy; this is true, to a certain extent, but considering how well the Prussians had marched under the self-same conditions, and the urgency of the situation, Grouchy might have made much more progress.

Excelmans, arriving at Sauvenière at six o'clock in the evening, sent out Bonnemains' Brigade (4th and 12th Dragoons) towards Sart à Walhain, and the 15th Dragoons towards Perwez, to reconnoitre. Scouts were also sent towards Tourinnes and Nil St Vincent. These scouts found a small Prussian rear-guard at Tourinnes, but they only watched the enemy for an hour, and then returned. Bonnemains brought his Brigade back to Ernage, where he bivouacked for the night. He had gathered information that the Prussians were retreating towards Wavre; and the 15th Dragoons also reported from the neighbourhood of Perwez to the same effect; so that Excelmans, at 10 P.M., knew with comparative certainty that the enemy were marching on Wavre.

Pajol, in the meantime, finding that he was mistaken in his conclusions as to the direction of the Prussian retreat, marched back from St Denis with Soult's Light Cavalry and Teste's Division to Le Mazy, the point from which he had started in the morning. Now, even if he had found that he was striking in a wrong direction, there can be no possible reason for his retreating to Le Mazy. He must have known that such a move, whether right or wrong, would have a very great influence on Grouchy's plan; therefore, instead of marching all his forces back, he should have sent an aide-de-camp or galloper to find where the main body was, or to find Grouchy and get fresh instructions. Pajol exercised no discretion whatever in making such a move.

At 10 P.M., at Gembloux, Grouchy wrote the following despatch to the Emperor:—

"GEMBLOUX, 17th June, 10 P.M.

"SIRE,—I have the honour to report to you that I occupy Gembloux and that my Cavalry is at Sauvenière.[1] The enemy, about 30,000 strong, continues his retreat. We have captured here a convoy of 400 cattle, magazines and baggage.

"It would appear, according to all the reports, that, on reaching Sauvenière, the Prussians divided into two columns: one of which must have taken the road to Wavre, passing by Sart à Walhain; the other would appear to have been directed on Perwez.

"It may perhaps be inferred from this that one portion is going to join Wellington; and that the centre, which is Blucher's army, is retreating on Liège. Another column, with artillery, having retreated by Namur,[2] General Excelmans has orders to push, this evening, six squadrons to Sart à Walhain, and three to Perwez. According to their report, if the mass of the Prussians is retiring on Wavre, I shall follow them in that direction, so as to prevent them from reaching Brussels, and to separate them from Wellington. If, on the contrary, my information proves that the principal Prussian force has marched on Perwez, I shall pursue the enemy by that town.

"Generals Thielemann and Borstel (?) formed part of the army which Your Majesty defeated yesterday; they were still here at 10 o'clock

---

[1] This would mislead Napoleon, who would infer that Pajol's Cavalry was included.

[2] Grouchy infers this from Pajol's capture of the Horse Battery near Le Mazy.

this morning,[1] and have announced that they have 20,000 casualties. They enquired on leaving, the distances of Wavre, Perwez, and Hannut. Blucher has been slightly wounded in the arm, but it has not prevented him from continuing to command after having had his wound dressed. He has not passed by Gembloux.—I am, with respect, Sire, Your Majesty's faithful subject, MARSHAL COUNT GROUCHY."

This despatch would not give Napoleon a very correct idea of the state of affairs. No mention was made by Grouchy of Pajol's detachment, so the Emperor could only infer that Grouchy had all his cavalry together and all his infantry together. Mention should have been made, too, of the discovery that the Prussians had not retreated by the Namur road. So far as could be learnt from this despatch, only 30,000 Prussians had been accounted for. That Blucher had "not passed through Gembloux" would at once suggest that he had gone by some other road, not explored by Grouchy, with his main body.

Grouchy's orders to his commanders for the next day, sent out at 10 P.M., showed that he still firmly believed that the Prussians were retreating on Liège, although in his despatch

---

[1] Grouchy seems to have avoided telling Napoleon that they were still there at two o'clock in the afternoon!

to Napoleon, he had recognised the possibility of their having taken the road to Wavre.

He ordered Excelmans' Cavalry and Vandamme's Corps to march to Sart à Walhain; Gérard's Corps to follow Vandamme's to Sart à Walhain, and the Seventh Cavalry Division to push on to Grand Leez; Pajol's force to march from Le Mazy to Grand Leez. (Pajol had reached St Denis, half-way from Le Mazy to Grand Leez, on the 17th, so that he now had covered this ground twice.)

When Bonnemain's reports to Excelmans reached Grouchy, he should have had no longer any doubts as to the true line of Blucher's retreat. Towards half-past two in the morning, news from Walhain came in, to the effect that the peasants there had reported that about three Prussian Corps had passed through on the previous day, marching in the direction of Wavre. A glance at the map will show that Gembloux to Walhain is in the direction of Wavre, and not of Liège. Further, from information gathered by the peasants from Prussian stragglers and the gossips who seem to find a place in every army, the enemy were talking of the coming battle near Brussels. As to Grouchy's thoughts, and the influence these reports had on him, it is difficult to find what train of reasoning he followed. He knew that Napoleon expected to fight Wellington near the Forest of Soignies: he knew, too, that the Emperor was anxious for him to prevent the Prussians from marching across to join the English, yet he did not consider the very great possibility that Blucher might rapidly join Wellington by a short flank march from Wavre. Had such a possibility entered his mind, he must have reflected on the best means of thwarting it, ere it became too late. Obviously his only move then was to make for the bridges at Moustier and Ottignies, *viâ* Saint Géry. By reaching the left bank of the Dyle (which he could easily do before Blucher), Grouchy could have either manœuvred to join Napoleon, when an addition of 33,000 troops must have overwhelmed Wellington, or he could have continued to pursue the Prussians, should it happen that he had been wrong in supposing that they were marching to join the English. It did not require extraordinary foresight or mental effort to realize how much more useful and how much more effective a move *viâ* St Géry and Moustier and the left bank of the Dyle would have been. If Grouchy was really as undecided as he appears to have been, as to the Prussian line of retreat, he should have had recourse to a movement which offered no doubtful advantages. A move across the Dyle by Moustier would have had a very great effect, and if the Prussians had really retreated on Liège, this movement of Grouchy's would still have its advantages. He could have thrown his weight into the fight at Waterloo; Napoleon would not blame him for this assistance, if he knew that the Prussians were out of reach.

At 6 A.M. on the morning of the 18th, Grouchy sent another message to Napoleon, stating that further information had been received, which confirmed the news that Blucher was making for Brussels "*viâ* Wavre, so as to concentrate there, or to give battle after joining Wellington." Grouchy told Napoleon in his message that he was "starting immediately for Wavre." But he himself did not actually start until 9 A.M.

He ordered Vandamme to march at 6 A.M., and Gérard at 8 A.M. Now, at that time of year, it was light enough to march at 3.30 A.M., hence Grouchy wasted another valuable two and a half hours, when time was all-important. Again, there was no necessity to keep Gérard's Corps waiting for Vandamme's to get ahead, as there were no less than four roads from Gembloux towards Corbaix, and the two inner ones could easily have been used for this march.

But the troops were still further delayed. Their breakfasts were not ready for them, and Vandamme's Corps did not start until nearly eight o'clock. They had had twelve hours in bivouac at Gembloux, and yet their breakfasts could not be ready by 6 A.M.! Excelmans' men at Sauvenière, too, were not in the saddle until 6 A.M. Grouchy himself left Gembloux at 8.30 A.M. He overtook Vandamme's Corps at Walhain at about 10 A.M., and here he dismounted for breakfast, allowing the troops to march on. At half-past ten, Excelmans' advanced guard came into touch with Thielemann's rear-guard, on the road to Wavre near La Baraque. This news was sent back to Grouchy, while Excelmans extended his men and engaged the Prussians lightly. At Walhain, Gérard, having ridden ahead of his troops, joined Grouchy, and during their breakfast, the sound of heavy firing in the direction of Mont St Jean was heard from the garden of the house where they had stopped. (This was the opening cannonade of the battle of Waterloo, which began at half-past eleven.)

Gérard at once urged Grouchy to change his direction and march to the sound of the cannonade. But Grouchy refused to take the responsibility of disobeying the orders he had received from Napoleon—"to pursue and attack the Prussians, and on no account to lose sight of them." Having received, a few minutes before, Excelmans' report from the front, he considered that he was moving in the right direction. To march across country to join Napoleon would have been contrary to his orders. To send a part of his forces across the Dyle would be to separate his army at a most dangerous moment. But this was just one of those cases when instructions need not have been implicitly obeyed. Circumstances had altered considerably since Grouchy had received his orders from Napoleon. A resolute and capable commander, in Grouchy's place, would have marched with his whole force by St Géry and Moustier from Gembloux at daybreak on the 18th. Certainly it would have been a mistake to divide his army at this time, but Grouchy should without doubt have taken upon himself the responsibility of digressing from his original instructions, and he would have been justified by the change in circumstances.

At the same time, while blaming Grouchy for his want of foresight and boldness, it must not be forgotten that the state of the roads and of the whole countryside was a very heavy factor against him. It was almost impossible to get the guns through the mud and mire which composed the roads. The infantry had to wade ankle-deep in many places, and for wheeled transport the roads were nearly impassable. Rain had fallen incessantly. Still, much could have been done by the cavalry, which was the arm which should have been relied upon most during these operations; and if the infantry had taken to the fields on either side of the road, they would hardly have marched slower than Vandamme's men. The Prussians, who were under the necessity of taking with them all their guns, waggons, and trains that they wished to save from the enemy on the same roads that their infantry used, were able to cover nearly $2\frac{1}{2}$ miles an hour. It might be presumed that the French could cover 2 miles an hour.

Vandamme, continuing his march while Grouchy breakfasted at leisure at Walhain, reached Nil St Vincent with his corps at 10.30 A.M. Here, in accordance with Grouchy's orders on the previous evening, he halted, and awaited fresh instructions. It was one o'clock before Grouchy arrived in person, and gave them to him. Then he and Excelmans, who had met with a Prussian rear-guard near Neuf Sart and La Baraque, were ordered to continue their march on Wavre. An hour later, Vandamme's advanced guard was attacked by Ledebur's detachment of Hussars, which had been left at Mont St Guibert. Ledebur had remained at Mont St Guibert, unaware of the proximity of the French, until his patrols caught sight of the troops at Nil St Vincent. Then he was alive to the dangers of his situation; for he was indeed in peril of being cut off. Excelmans' Dragoons at La Baraque stood across his rear, and Vandamme's Corps was threatening to cut off his retreat by Corbaix. He, however, was a man of great military instinct, and saw that his only chance of escape lay in attacking the French advanced squadrons. This he did with his Hussars, and, being reinforced from Pirch's Corps by two battalions, which in addition to the battalions which were with him before, made up his detachment to the strength of a brigade, he boldly attacked the head of Vandamme's column. Grouchy ordered Excelmans to turn Ledebur's position by Dion-le-Mont, but before the French Cavalry had developed their movement, the Prussians had retreated through the wood of La Huzelle and had fallen back on Wavre. Vandamme was sent off in pursuit, with orders to follow the Prussians to Wavre, take up a position there, and await instructions.

Grouchy himself, as soon as Ledebur had retired, rode off to Limelette, a village on the left bank of the Dyle, to reconnoitre with his own eyes. It is a pity, for his reputation as a

General, that he had not taken upon himself more of this essential duty, during these operations. At Limelette, he heard very plainly the distant roar of the guns at Mont St Jean, and he had no longer any doubts that a big battle was in progress on his left. On his return to La Baraque, towards 4 P.M., he received a letter from Napoleon, written at Le Caillou farm-house at 10 A.M., in which the Emperor ordered him to push on to Wavre, at the same time drawing nearer to the main army, and keeping up the closest communication by Ottignies and Moustier. This letter had the unfortunate effect of confirming Grouchy in his own ideas of the correctness of his movements, while he made no alterations in his dispositions of Gérard's and Vandamme's Corps to bring them nearer the Emperor. But he did order Pajol, who had reported from Grand Leez that no trace of the Prussians had been found between that place and Tourinnes, to take his cavalry and Teste's Division across country to Limale, on the Dyle, where he was to force a passage.

This order given, Grouchy rode off towards Wavre, where the impatient Vandamme was already beginning an attack.

CHAPTER V

BLUCHER MARCHES TOWARDS MONT ST JEAN WITH THE FIRST, SECOND, AND FOURTH CORPS.

AT nightfall on the 17th, while Grouchy was still at Gembloux, the whole of Blucher's army (except two Divisions, the Ninth and Thirteenth, and the Reserve Cavalry of Thielemann's Corps, which were posted as rear-guards to the Third and Fourth Corps) had reached Wavre and its neighbourhood. As explained in the third chapter, the Second and Third Corps bivouacked on the left bank of the Dyle, beyond Wavre, and the First and Fourth on the right bank. Pirch I. was between St Anne and Aisemont; Bulow was at Dion-le-Mont. The rear-guards were posted at Vieux Sart and Mont St Guibert; these troops fell back next day as the French advanced. On Blucher's left, patrols scoured the country towards Namur and Louvain; on his right they watched the Dyle and its approaches. Limale was held by a detachment from Zieten's Corps to protect the right flank, and cavalry patrols rode to and fro over all the valley of the Dyle. The reserve ammunition columns with full supplies reached Wavre in the afternoon of the 17th, and thus all the batteries were replenished. It speaks well for the Prussian arrangements that these supplies should have reached Wavre at so important a moment; when on account of their unexpected retreat to Wavre, all previous arrangements had to be cancelled.

It was only when Blucher had thus made sure of his concentration and of the refilling of his waggons and limbers, that he replied to Wellington:—

"I shall not come with two corps only, but with my whole army; upon this understanding, however, that, should the French not attack us on the 18th, we shall attack them on the 19th."

Having reached Wavre in safety, the Prussians, though they had lost none of their courage, began to feel greater confidence. The defeat at Ligny had merely damped their ardour for a space; it had in nowise impaired their fighting value. The men were eager for a further trial with the French, and they were now more determined than before to regain prestige and humble the victors of Jena. Nevertheless, among the lesser troops and the newly raised corps from the Rhenish provinces, there had been many desertions. Most of these had once been French soldiers themselves, and knew the fear of Napoleon. To the number of 8000 these men "absented" themselves after the battle of Ligny, while some fled headlong to Liège. On the whole, considering the heterogeneous composition of Blucher's army, there was very little bad faith among the men.

About midnight on the 17th, a message from Wellington, through Muffling, reached Blucher. It ran:—

"The Anglo-Allied army is posted with its right upon Braine l'Alleud, its centre upon Mont St Jean, and its left upon La Haye; with the enemy in front. The Duke awaits the attack, but calculates on Prussian support."

Gneisenau was very suspicious of the sincerity of Wellington's intentions; he believed that the Duke would fall back at the last moment, and involve the Prussian army in a serious disaster. But Blucher had a greater idea of the honour of the words of generals, and finally overcame the reluctance of his Chief of the Staff. He thereupon replied to Wellington that—

"Bulow's Corps will set off marching tomorrow at daybreak in your direction. It will be immediately followed by the Second Corps. The First and Third Corps will also hold themselves in readiness to proceed towards you. The exhaustion of the troops, part of whom have not yet arrived, does not allow of my commencing my movement earlier."

An order to this effect was at once sent to Bulow at Dion-le-Mont:—

"You will, therefore, at daybreak, march with the Fourth Corps from Dion-le-Mont, through Wavre, in the direction of Chapelle St Lambert, on nearing which you will conceal your force as much as possible, in case the enemy should not, by that time, be seriously engaged with the Duke of Wellington; but should it be otherwise, you will make a most vigorous attack on the enemy's right flank. The Second Corps will follow you as a direct support; the First and Third will also be held in readiness to move in the same direction if necessary. You will leave a detachment in observation at Mont St Guibert; which, if pressed, will gradually fall back on Wavre. All the baggage train, and everything not actually required in the field, will be sent to Louvain."

Now, why was Bulow's Corps, which was at Dion-le-Mont, to lead the flank march, while Pirch I., Zieten, and Thielemann were all so much nearer to Chapelle St Lambert? Dion-le-Mont was 10 miles by road from Chapelle St Lambert; Aisemont, where Pirch was, was 8 miles; Bierges, Zieten's headquarters, was only 4 miles; and La Bavette, Thielemann's headquarters, 6 miles. It followed, then, that Pirch could not move until Bulow's Corps had passed. Had Blucher's men been so exhausted, it would have saved most of them many miles of weary marching if Zieten and Thielemann had been ordered to Chapelle St

Lambert, and Pirch and Bulow to move in nearer to Wavre. Bulow's Corps had so far taken no part in the fighting, and it may have been Blucher's desire to give them opportunities, but for all that he knew Wellington might be in dire straits as soon as the battle began, so that he should not have hesitated to send off the nearest Corps.

Bulow commenced his march from Dion-le-Mont at daybreak, with Losthin's Fifteenth Division as advanced guard. At 7 A.M. the Division reached Wavre, but the crossing of the bridges over the Dyle occupied a long time, and the passage through the town was hindered by a disastrous fire which broke out in the main street, through which the troops were marching. Great excitement prevailed, as it was feared that all the reserve ammunition waggons, parked in the town, were in danger. But the troops of the 14th Regiment of the line made great exertions, and were able to overcome the flames. But the Corps had been delayed for two valuable hours, and did not clear Wavre until 10 A.M. Meanwhile, parties of cavalry were busy reconnoitring towards Maransart and Couture. A detachment of Hussars rode out to patrol the valley of the Lasne, and another detachment to establish communication with Ledebur at Mont St Guibert.

All the country between Plancenoit and the Dyle was carefully examined, and reports were sent in continually. The Prussian scouting work was very efficiently performed, and is still worthy of notice, even in these days. Every opportunity was taken of searching and feeling for the enemy. Not only were the Prussians accurately informed, but they hindered Napoleon's communications with Grouchy, by occupying the roads their messengers might use, and compelling them to make very wide détours.

The roads being reported clear, Bulow's Corps continued on its way, but progress was not rapid, owing to the state of the roads and the exhaustion of the troops. The advanced guard reached St Lambert at about 10.30 A.M., and the main body arrived about mid-day, but the rear-guard (Ryssel's Division) did not arrive until three o'clock in the afternoon. At Maransart, the reconnoitring party found that the French had no detachments watching their flank, and the valley of the Lasne was clear.

The safe arrival of Bulow's Corps at St Lambert, and the reports from his scouts, made Blucher resolve to hasten the march of the First and Second Corps. Pirch's men had broken up their bivouacs at 5 A.M., but had had to wait until 12 noon to allow Bulow's Corps to pass clear of

Wavre. Zieten, on the left bank of the Dyle, marched for Ohain at noon. Blucher was uneasy about Grouchy's strength, and his intenttions. He was anxious to take his whole army towards Mont St Jean, but he was afraid of an attack on his rear and flank. He therefore determined to leave Thielemann's Corps at Wavre to await Grouchy's approach, and if the French were not in strength, Thielemann was to march to join the main body, leaving a small force in Wavre as a rear-guard. Blucher himself, leaving Gneisenau to arrange matters at Wavre, rode on to St Lambert at 11 A.M.

While Pirch's Corps was passing through Wavre, Ledebur's detachment retired on the town from Mont St Guibert, and the enemy's cavalry appeared in sight. This was not a pleasant time for action, as the troops were thickly crowded in the defiles and lanes. Sohr's Brigade of Cavalry, forming Pirch's rear-guard, fell back, and the Seventh and Eighth Divisions were halted and faced round. The Eighth Division was posted in the wood of La Huzelle, with the Seventh in support. But the French did not press their advance, and at three o'clock, the Prussians retired across the Dyle. Pirch's Corps then continued its march on St Lambert, leaving Thielemann in defence of Wavre.

As a flank march, Blucher's movement to St Lambert was both a tactical and a strategical success; although under different circumstances, it would have been a failure. For Grouchy should never have allowed it to be carried out. By efficient reconnoitring, such as was carried out by the Prussian Hussars, Grouchy should have discovered the threatened movement early in the morning of the 18th, and have sent Maurin's Cavalry Division, followed by Excelmans' Cavalry and Gérard's Corps, to Moustier and Ottignies. The cavalry could have reached the bridges there in time to threaten Blucher's flank, and prevent him, if not from assisting Wellington with a part of his forces, at least from throwing his whole weight into the battle against Napoleon. And even at the end, Grouchy might, had he been too late across the Dyle to prevent Blucher from joining Wellington, have covered Napoleon's retreat, and saved the Emperor's army from the disastrous rout which befell it.

CHAPTER VI

THIELEMANN'S INSTRUCTIONS AND HIS DISPOSITIONS AT WAVRE

THIELEMANN had been ordered by Blucher to defend Wavre at all costs if the French appeared in force, but if there was no fear of a serious attack, to leave a small rear-guard there and follow the other three Corps.

As Excelmans' Cavalry had shown so little activity in their attack on the outposts, Thielemann, towards three o'clock, decided to move his Corps towards Ohain, leaving only a small detachment to defend Wavre. In his judgment, if the French had meant to hinder the march towards Wellington, they would have appeared in force several hours ago. So slowly did they appear to be approaching, and in no great numbers, that Thielemann had every reason to suppose that a small force would be sufficient to cover his march, and that his main body would be of much greater assistance at St Lambert than at Wavre. His patrols had so far only seen the opposing cavalry and the head of Vandamme's Corps; the whole strength of Grouchy's force was as yet undiscovered. Accordingly, at about 3.30 P.M., the Ninth, Tenth, Eleventh, and Twelfth Divisions, with the Reserve Cavalry and Artillery, were ordered to begin marching towards Frischermont and Chapelle St Lambert; and a small detachment under Colonel Zeppelin, consisting of the two Fusilier battalions of the 30th Regiment of the Line and the 1st Kurmark Landwehr Regiment, belonging to the Ninth Division, was detailed to hold Wavre.

When, at 4 P.M., the head of Vandamme's Corps appeared on the road from La Baraque leading towards the main bridge at Wavre, and Excelmans' Cavalry was seen massing at Dion-le-Mont, one Division, the Twelfth (Stulpnagel's) was already on the road to Rixensart, and the Eleventh was in the act of marching. The Ninth Division (Borcke's), which had been posted near the farm of La Huzelle, fell back before Vandamme, but on reaching Wavre, it was found that the bridges had been barricaded, and no entry was possible. This left the Division in a situation of some danger, but Borcke led his men off to the right, to Basse Wavre, where there was another bridge, about half a mile down the stream. Here they crossed, and destroyed the bridge behind them. This was a most necessary step, because

Excelmans' Dragoons were scarcely a mile and a half away at Dion-le-Mont, and they might at any moment make a dash for Basse Wavre. The destruction of the bridge, too, saved Thielemann the task of defending it, and so scattering his troops, which were already none too numerous. To have left the bridge as a means of possible counter-attack was not desirable, nor even necessary, as a counter-attack by Limale or the Mill of Bierges would have had all the points in its favour.

Having no further orders, Borcke lined the left bank of the Dyle at Basse Wavre with picked marksmen from the 8th Regiment of the Line and the 1st Battalion of the 30th Regiment. These he placed under the command of Major Dittfurth, who had already distinguished himself during the close of the battle at Ligny. These skirmishers extended from Basse Wavre to Wavre, and took cover behind the trees lining the bank, and the neighbouring hedges and walls. Borcke continued his way to Wavre, and there detached one battalion (the 2nd of the 30th Regiment) and two squadrons of cavalry, to reinforce Colonel Zeppelin's detachment, which, by this time, had loopholed all the buildings along the bank of the river, and were improvising defences. This done, Borcke resumed his march towards the main Prussian army!

General Borcke's timely reinforcements to Zeppelin, and his prompt initiative in lining the Dyle at Basse Wavre with sharpshooters, afterwards proved to be of the greatest assistance. There was nothing but his own foresight to cause him to take these measures as he passed along, and it was fortunate for Thielemann that he did not march off without detaching these parties.

As soon as Vandamme's Corps plainly showed signs of attacking, Thielemann immediately halted all his Divisions and began to dispose them for defence.

The position afforded favourable means for defence. The Dyle, ordinarily a shallow stream, but at this time in flood, owing to the heavy rains, ran along the front in a narrow valley. The town of Wavre, situated on the left bank, extended for about half a mile along the stream, and was connected with a few buildings which formed a kind of suburb on the opposite bank, by two stone bridges, one of which, the larger of the two, carried the main Brussels-Namur road. About three-quarters of a mile up-stream, on the left bank, was the Mill of Bierges, destined to be the scene of the fiercest fighting; here there was a wooden bridge, carrying a narrow country road, leading from the village of Bierges. At Limale, a village $2\frac{1}{4}$ miles up-stream from Wavre, and at Limelette, another village a mile further, there were also wooden bridges. On the right bank of the Dyle, there was a series of hills commanding the town, the river, and the bridges. On the left bank, a similar series of heights, rather steeper but not so high; and numerous hedges, lanes, and hollows on the left bank compensated for the greater "command" of the ground on the opposite side of the stream. All the buildings along the river were hastily loop-holed, and the two bridges at Wavre strongly barricaded. Basse Wavre included a few buildings about half a mile below Wavre; and houses stood on both banks. There were many lanes and cross-roads branching from the main Brussels road, on both sides of the stream, so that the movements of troops could be conducted generally under cover; but the state of the roads was so bad, that any movement at all was extremely difficult and slow. Grouchy's side commanded Thielemann's, but the latter's was well covered, both from artillery and musket fire. Behind Wavre was a hill, which would afford good cover for reserves.

Thielemann saw that the enemy might attack at any or all of the points of passage: and he was therefore determined to be prepared for any emergency. In placing the troops, his one idea was to hold the line of the stream with skirmishers and sharpshooters in sufficient strength to prevent any sudden surprise, and to keep his supports together close at hand, to reinforce any threatened point or to guard his flanks. He placed the Tenth Division (Kampfen's) behind Wavre, resting on a small wood near the Brussels road. The Twelfth Division (Stulpnagel's), which had started on its way to St Lambert, was brought back to Bierges, and placed behind the village. The bridge at Bierges was barricaded, and the mill prepared for defence. One battery of Horse Artillery (No. 20) was placed in front of the village. The Eleventh Division (Luck's) was placed astride the Brussels road, behind Wavre, and on the left of the Tenth Division.

The Ninth Division (Borcke's) was to have been placed in rear of the Tenth and Eleventh Divisions as a general reserve, but Borcke, after detaching the troops to hold Basse Wavre and reinforce Zeppelin, had marched his Division off towards the main army, in the belief that the whole Corps had already marched. As Borcke had made a wide détour from Basse Wavre to La Bavette, there was some reason for his misjudgment. His march was not discovered in time; so Thielemann's force was reduced by six battalions and one battery of artillery.

Hobe's Cavalry Division (Marwitz's and

Lottum's Brigades) was posted with one battery of Horse Artillery (No. 18) near La Bavette: a central position, whence it might be directed on any part of the field. The remainder of the artillery was distributed along the front. The bank of the Dyle and the riverside buildings in Wavre were occupied by Light troops and sharpshooters from the different regiments. Two more companies of infantry were sent to Basse Wavre, under Major Bornstaedt, to reinforce the detachment there. Three battalions and three squadrons under Stengel, from Zieten's Corps, were sent back to guard the bridge at Limale.

In point of numbers, Thielemann's troops were less than half as strong as those of Grouchy; and it was evident that the coming fight was to be of the fiercest description. Thielemann's men were in fine trim and eager for the enemy's attack.

CHAPTER VII

THE BATTLE OF WAVRE

VANDAMME'S advanced guard, between three and four o'clock, had driven Borcke's Division back on Wavre, and Vandamme, eager to burst into activity after the irritable delays on the march, proceeded to attack without waiting for Gérard, or even for Grouchy's orders. He was afraid that night would come on and allow the Prussians to escape, as they had done from Sombreffe. He only saw in front of him a force waiting to be attacked; he had no thoughts for the general situation. He was a rough-and-ready soldier, and he thought he saw his chance of beating the Prussians single-handed. He longed for the marshal's bâton; he was jealous, too, of Gérard.

At this time, Excelmans was at Dion-le-Mont with his cavalry, slightly in rear of Vandamme. Gérard was nearing La Baraque, some 4 miles in rear. Pajol, with his cavalry and Teste's Division, had just reached Tourinnes.

Before Grouchy could reach Vandamme, the

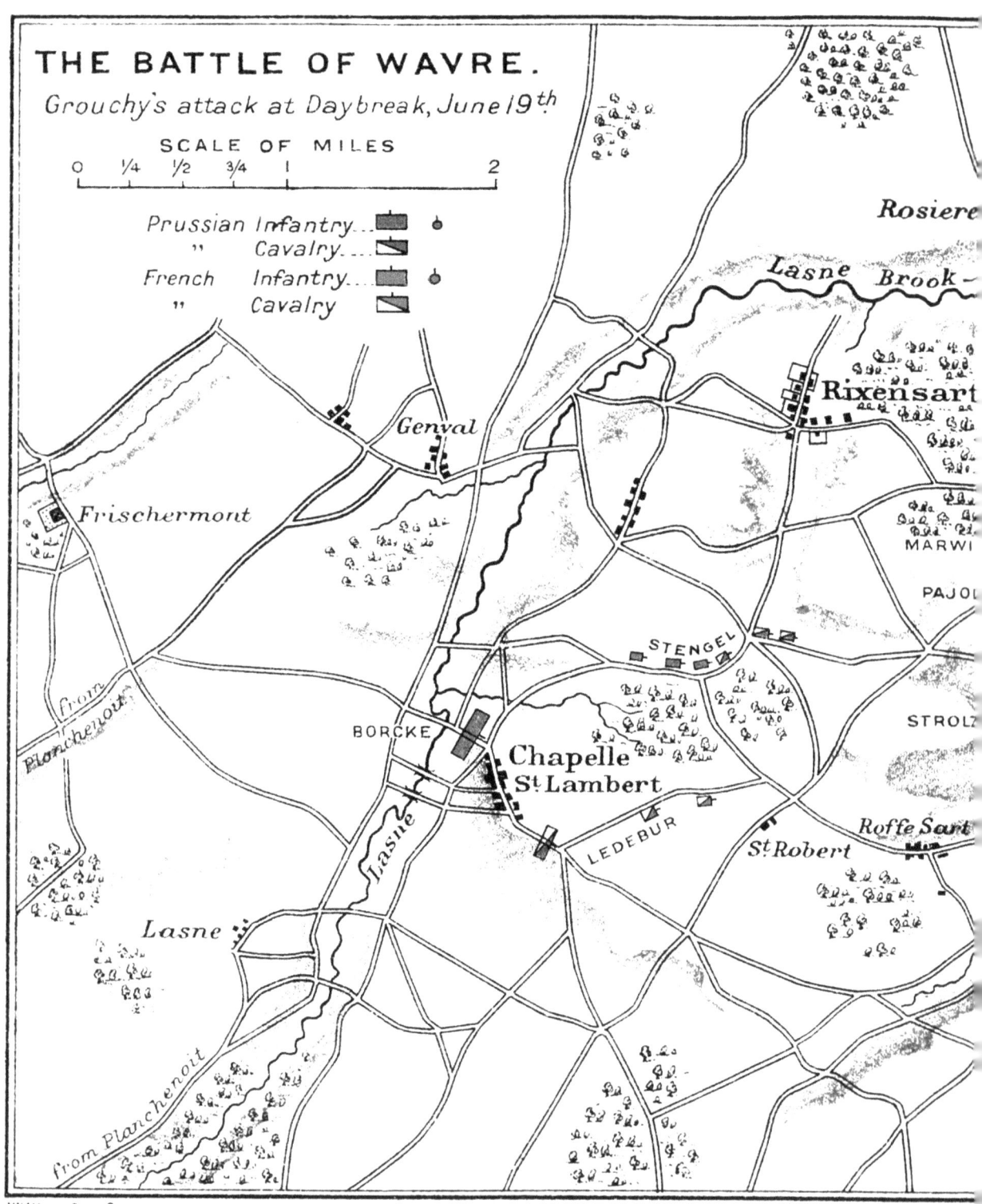

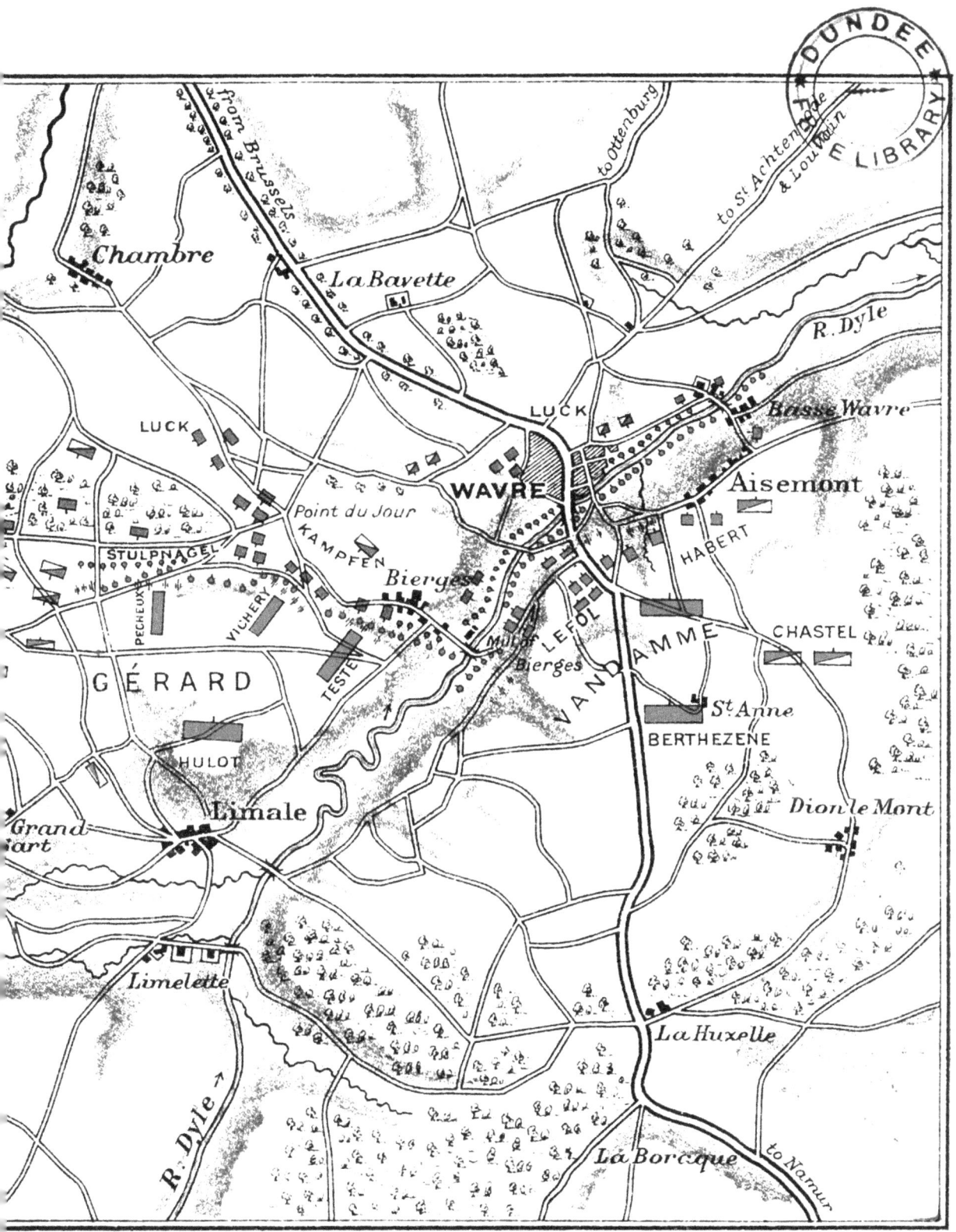

latter had launched the whole of his Tenth Division (Habert's), consisting of the 22nd, 34th, 70th and 88th Regiments of the Line, against the village opposite Wavre. The French, in heavy columns, supported by a furious cannonade from two batteries of twelve-pounders placed to the right of the Brussels road, cleared the few Prussian sharpshooters from the buildings, and pressed on to the main bridge. But here they were met with a terrible fire from their front and on their flanks, from the sharpshooters lining the hedges and buildings on the opposite bank. The Prussian batteries played fiercely on their columns, and on the whole of the ground behind them, where their own guns were placed. In a few minutes, General Habert and 600 men were down. Attempts to force the barricaded bridge were beaten back with frightful loss, and the Division was placed in a very serious position. If they retreated, they came under the heavy fire of the Prussian batteries on the opposite heights; if they remained where they stood, the enemy's sharpshooters would annihilate them; to advance was impossible. Gradually, they found shelter, company by company, under the walls of the buildings along the bank, whence they had just driven the Prussians. Vandamme was now deeply committed to the fight.

Grouchy, who had by this time arrived on the scene, unaware of the strength of the Prussians at Wavre, and unaware, too, of Blucher's march on St Lambert, made arrangements to support Vandamme's attack by two other attacks on either flank. For this purpose, he ordered Excelmans to move his cavalry from Dion-le-Mont to the front of Basse Wavre, and a battalion under Lefol to make an attempt to cross at the Mill of Bierges.

It was now five o'clock, and a message arrived from Napoleon, sent at 1.30 P.M., saying that Bulow's Corps had just been seen at St Lambert, and ordering Grouchy to lose no time in moving to join the Emperor's right, when he would crush Bulow in flank. Grouchy, knowing that he could not now disengage Vandamme, sent orders to Pajol to hasten his march on Limale, and ordered Gérard to lead the Fourth Corps towards that village at once. He conceived the idea of assaulting and carrying Wavre with Vandamme's Corps, aided afterwards by Excelmans' Cavalry, while he sent the remainder of his army on Chapelle St Lambert *viâ* Limale. This was a skilful project, and the best under the circumstances, no doubt; for the movement on Limale would have had the double effect of turning Thielemann's left flank, while it promised to bring a strong reinforcement on Napoleon's right. But it was now too late. The opportunity had passed much earlier in the day.

Hulot's Division, of Gérard's Corps, had now reached the scene of Vandamme's efforts, and Grouchy ordered it to move to the left and force a passage at the Mill of Bierges. Lefol's battalion had made several attempts to cross the bridges there, but had each time been beaten back by the Prussian sharpshooters and the batteries in front of Bierges village. Some guns were sent to aid Lefol and endeavour to silence the Prussian artillery opposite, but they were themselves outnumbered and silenced. On Hulot's arrival, a fresh battalion was sent to relieve Lefol's detachment, and the whole Division followed. By this time, both banks of the Dyle, from Bierges to Basse Wavre, were lined with skirmishers and sharpshooters, pouring a terrific fire into each other. Hulot's Division had great difficulty in moving through the swamps and mud to the bridge at Bierges, and suffered severely from the Prussian batteries. The battalion which relieved Lefol's began at once to make a fresh attempt to force the bridge, but was beaten off with loss.

Grouchy, impatient and fretful, rode off to meet the remainder of the Fourth Corps and Pajol's force, still some distance behind on the

Namur-Brussels road. Ordering Pajol to make all haste for Limale, he returned to the field, where he found that matters had made no progress. Infuriated by the repeated failures to carry the bridge and Mill of Bierges, he himself led a fresh attack with Hulot's men, but nothing could overcome the fire of the Prussians. Gérard fell wounded and was carried off the field.

Finding his attacks on Bierges and Wavre unsuccessful, Grouchy left Vandamme and Excelmans to carry on the fight, while he himself led the remainder of Gérard's Corps to Limale. Pajol had arrived in front of the Limale bridge shortly before dark, with Teste's Division and his own cavalry. Stengel, who held Limale with three battalions and three squadrons, had omitted to barricade the bridge, and when Pajol perceived this he sent a regiment of Hussars at full speed on the bridge, and, charging four abreast only, these horsemen burst through the Prussians posted at the farther end. The passage was forced and Teste's Division was sent across; and Stengel, finding himself very much outnumbered, abandoned Limale and took up a position on the heights above the village. Hearing of Stengel's difficulties, Thielemann sent the Twelfth Division (Stulpnagel's) and Hobe's Cavalry to reinforce him. Thielemann saw now that the real point of crossing was Limale, and not Bierges or Basse Wavre, and he moved all the troops he could spare towards his right. Four battalions of the Tenth Division took up Stulpnagel's former position, and three battalions of the Twelfth Division were left to defend Bierges; the remainder marched to join Stengel.

It was now dark, but the battle continued with vigour. Grouchy posted his battalions in front of Limale, and, considering the darkness of the night, it is surprising how he managed to place them without confusion. Stengel's men kept up a harassing fire on his columns as they wound their way through the muddy lanes from the village to the height above the Dyle and deployed to receive Stulpnagel's attack. Pajol moved his cavalry to the French left flank.

Stulpnagel, his Division now reduced to six battalions, left one battalion (the Fusilier battalion of the 5th Kurmark Landwehr Regiment) and one battery in a copse north of Bierges, as a reserve, and joined Stengel, who was now on his right, with his remaining five battalions. His orders were to endeavour to regain Limale, and drive the French across the Dyle. He formed his attack with two battalions in first line, with three in support. His two squadrons were sent to reinforce Stengel, and the rest of the cavalry posted in rear, to be in readiness for a flank movement. The darkness was so great that little cohesion was possible between the units, and it is not surprising that the attack fell to pieces. The formation of the ground was unknown, and the little folds and features which make or mar a night attack were plentiful: and unfortunately for the Prussians, they marred their plans. As the front line was advancing in fair order, a hollow lane was suddenly met with, and caused great confusion, being unexpected; but worse than this, the opposite side was lined with French sharpshooters, who poured volleys across into the disordered Prussians. There was, for a time, no attempt to seek cover, and the losses from the fire of the French opposite were heavy, in spite of the darkness. The second line, which was to have supported the first, moved too far to its left, and became itself a front line, engaging more French skirmishers. Stengel, on the right, was charged by cavalry and compelled to retire.

Stulpnagel perceived that little good could come of an attack the successive steps of which had merged into a confused line, and resolved to withdraw to the shelter of the wood behind Point-du-Jour, leaving a line of outposts to watch the front edge. The cavalry took post behind the infantry; and the French fearing to venture through the uncertainties of the night, the fighting on this side ceased.

Meanwhile, on the Prussian left, before Wavre and the Mill of Bierges, the fighting went on most vigorously. The darkness did not prevent the fury of the fight; it only seemed to add to the grimness of it. The whole of Vandamme's Corps was now engaged, and time after time the French rushed at the barricades on the bridges. Thirteen separate assaults were beaten back by the Prussians, and no less than five times the defenders, in pursuing the routed enemy, attacked and drove them from the houses on the far side of the Dyle. Once, the French had possession of the main bridge, and had even occupied some of the neighbouring buildings, but the Prussian reserves were hurried up, and these drove out the French. Each time there seemed a chance of the enemy obtaining a footing on the left bank, the Prussian reserves, judiciously posted near at hand among the side-streets and dwellings, rushed out and overwhelmed the intruders. Four battalions defended Wavre against the whole of Vandamme's Corps. But while the attackers were exposed at each attempt to cross the bridges, the defenders were secure behind their loop-holed walls. Only a great superiority of artillery fire, to prepare the way for the assault, and to destroy some of the nearer walls, could have made a crossing successful. A few daring Sappers might have brought up bags of powder to blow in the barricades; they could only have done so by sacrificing themselves, but heroes and brave men were not wanting. Shortage of powder, however, explains the fact that no such attempt was made.

At Basse Wavre, lower down the stream, the attack had not been pressed. Excelmans' Cavalry had been ordered to make a demonstration on that flank, but cavalry cannot cross a stream without bridge or ford. Only one French battalion, supported by a single gun and two squadrons, had shown themselves, and these were of no use without a bridge to carry them across.

The only advantage which Grouchy had obtained was on his left, which had rolled back the Prussian right, but had in no way destroyed it. Firing ceased at about 11 P.M., and great preparations were made on both sides for a renewal of the fight at daybreak. But Grouchy was well pleased with his success on the left, since he assumed that he had at least cut off half of the Prussian army. It was now too late for him to be of assistance to Napoleon, and the din of the distant battle had long ago died out. But Grouchy took no steps to ascertain how matters stood with the Emperor. He merely sent orders to Vandamme to bring his Corps across the Dyle at Limale, as he intended making an end of the Prussian right flank, and marching to join Napoleon before Brussels, thinking, for a reason which cannot be explained, that the allies had been beaten. Perhaps it was his confident belief in the invincibility of the Emperor; but yet again he made no efforts to gain information or to confirm his own views. Teste's Division came up during the night, and, crossing the Dyle at Limale, took post on the right flank of Gérard's Corps, between Limale and Bierges, and resting its own right flank on the Dyle.

Thielemann, on the other hand, had sent an officer's patrol to reconnoitre on his right, and to ascertain what had occurred at Mont St Jean. This officer returned during the night with the news of Napoleon's rout, and consequently Thielemann expected Grouchy, who, he supposed, was fully acquainted with the situation, to retreat early next morning, if not during the night. But two incidents occurred which sadly reduced his numbers and which caused a rearrangement of his troops. Stengel, for a reason never yet explained, calmly marched off from Stulpnagel's right at daybreak, to St Lambert, there to join his own Corps, Zieten's. Possibly he had personal views of the situation, and considered the battle over! It is uncharitable to suppose that he had feelings against Thielemann or Stulpnagel. But in either or any case, his conduct was most blameworthy and most unsoldierlike. His departure (which must have been noticed before his movement had gone far, and therefore could have been prevented) reduced Thielemann's force by three battalions and three squadrons; and this at a moment when every man was of importance. But even another inexplicable movement was made by Colonel Ledebur, who, with his detachment of five squadrons and two guns of the Horse Artillery, marched to St Lambert during Grouchy's attack, bivouacked there for the night, and then moved off to join the Fourth Corps on the 19th. These two detachments were thus of no use whatever to Thielemann, and their extraordinary action must have caused him considerable anxiety, since it might have appeared as desertion. But Thielemann was firm in his belief that Grouchy would retreat, and when, at daybreak on June 19, he saw French troops still in their positions, he assumed that they were merely acting as a rear-guard to cover the general retirement. He therefore ordered

Colonel Marwitz, with the 8th Uhlans and two squadrons of the 6th Kurmark Landwehr Cavalry, to attack Grouchy's left flank above Limale, while Hobe, with the 5th and 7th Uhlans, was to advance in support on Marwitz's left. To replace Stengel's detachment, the Twelfth Division was extended still further to its right, weakening the whole of its front line, and leaving only three battalions in reserve in the wood near Point-du-Jour. On Stulpnagel's left, six battalions of the Tenth Division held the line to Bierges and the Dyle. In support, there were three battalions of the 3rd Kurmark Landwehr Regiment, from the Eleventh Division, while the 4th Kurmark Landwehr (two battalions) with two squadrons, were posted behind Wavre as a general reserve. Two battalions from the Twelfth Division were posted to hold the Mill of Bierges. The remainder of Thielemann's force was extended along the Dyle in Wavre and Basse Wavre; but little fighting on this front was now expected.

To support Marwitz's attack, two batteries (one horse and one foot) opened fire on the French columns massed on the plateau above Limale, but the enemy's artillery, which was greatly superior, replied fiercely and soon silenced the Prussian guns, five of which were disabled.

Grouchy, who was still ignorant of Napoleon's defeat, prepared an attack on his part. His numbers vastly exceeded Thielemann's thin forces, and counted Gérard's Corps (three divisions), Teste's Division and Pajol's Cavalry. (Vandamme had not obeyed Grouchy's orders of the previous night, to march with his Corps to Limale.) Grouchy now formed three Divisions —Teste's, Vichery's and Pecheux's—in first line, divided into three columns of attack. Teste's Division formed the right column, and was to attack Bierges and the mill; Vichery's Division in the centre, to attack the Prussian centre; and Pecheux's Division against Stulpnagel's right flank. Each column was provided with a battery of artillery, escorted and preceded by skirmishers. The remaining division—Hulot's—was in reserve behind the centre column. Pajol's Cavalry was to turn the Prussian right flank, which rested on the wood of Rixensart. Twenty-eight French against ten Prussian battalions.

Thielemann perceived the coming attack, and reinforced his line with one battalion, which he posted on his left, and which was all he could spare. The French columns were too heavy for the Prussians, who were hopelessly outnumbered. The Twelfth Division gave way, and the French took the wood of Rixensart.

Stulpnagel fell back on his supports—the three battalions of the Eleventh Division and two batteries—and took up a new position behind the wood. Teste's attack on Bierges was stoutly opposed by the two battalions posted there, and four battalions of the Tenth Division were brought up in support. On the Prussian extreme right, the cavalry brigades of Marwitz and Lottum—in all, twelve squadrons—occupied Chambre and secured the flank.

At 8 A.M. definite news arrived of the French rout at Waterloo, and the Prussians were aroused to renew their efforts. The tidings had a great effect on the spirits of the men, and they rushed to the attack with great vigour, recapturing the wood of Rixensart. This counter-stroke deceived Grouchy, who at first believed that the Prussians had been reinforced; but Stulpnagel's effort was short-lived, and could not be pushed further, for want of supports. Consequently, Grouchy in his turn ordered a fresh attack, and the Prussians were again driven out of the wood. At 9 A.M. Bierges fell into the hands of Teste, who had had a very hard task to drive out the two gallant battalions defending the place. The capture of this point was a serious blow, for the French had now broken through Thielemann's defence at the angle; and it was no longer possible for the

Prussians to resist on both wings. The centre having been broken, and the right seriously threatened by overwhelming numbers, Thielemann could not but withdraw.

Vandamme had remained in front of Wavre, but had not attacked, although the defence had been greatly weakened by detachments for the right.

At 10 A.M. Thielemann ordered the retreat. He knew that Grouchy must himself retreat sooner or later, but to hold on to Wavre too long would mean Thielemann's own destruction. By retreating, he would gain time, and when the opportunity occurred, he would again advance, and possibly convert Grouchy's retirement into a rout. Under the protection of Marwitz's Cavalry —the 7th and 8th Uhlans, and the 3rd and 6th Landwehr Cavalry with three batteries of horse artillery — the infantry retired, and Zeppelin evacuated Wavre. The rear-guard, posting itself on the Brussels road, threatened the French left whenever an opportunity occurred.

As soon as Zeppelin withdrew from Wavre, Vandamme pushed his men across the Dyle, both at Bierges and Wavre, and advanced up the Brussels road. In rear of Wavre, in a hollow behind the town, two battalions of the 4th Kurmark Landwehr Regiment were posted, and these were compelled to fall back. But one of the battalions, reaching a small wood near La Bavette, re-formed, and attacked and drove back a squadron of French cavalry which was pursuing. The other battalion overthrew a French battalion, and then continued its retreat. Marwitz's Cavalry repulsed the squadrons at the head of Vandamme's columns, which were now advancing towards La Bavette by the main road and by a parallel lane on the left. The Prussian infantry retreated towards Louvain, through the villages of St Achtenrode and Ottenburg; but behind St Achtenrode, Thielemann halted and took up a defensive position. To retreat too far would hinder his plan of turning back again to attack Grouchy when he retired. The French, too, had halted about La Bavette, having at this moment heard definite news of Napoleon's disaster. No cavalry pursued the Prussians, for in the close and intersected country beyond La Bavette it was impossible for cavalry to manœuvre, and only with difficulty could it be traversed by infantry.

As to Borcke in the meantime, his Division had reached Couture at 8 P.M. on the previous evening, and a report was sent to Blucher. A reply was returned that Borcke was to remain at Couture and await further orders. But early next morning, hearing from Stengel, who had passed through St Lambert, that the French were following him, Borcke extended two of his battalions from St Robert to Rixensart, with the remaining four in reserve. He had an idea that the French were advancing in his direction, but had he only known the true position of Grouchy's troops, he might have been so bold as to attack them in rear. He certainly would have caused a panic among Grouchy's men, who would naturally suppose that Blucher was returning with the main body. But, seeing three French cavalry regiments detached to watch him, Borcke held back, and positively took no action, although the Prussians still held Wavre. What a diversion he might have made!

In the fighting of the 18th and 19th, Thielemann lost 2,500 men; the French about 2,200; and the results were very creditable to the Prussians. Attacked by more than double his numbers, and with very little time to prepare his defence, Thielemann had held off the French during all the critical hours of the afternoon and evening of the 18th. He had successfully occupied the whole of Grouchy's force during the time when the latter might still have been of use to Napoleon. Without knowing it, Grouchy had been almost surrounded, but Borcke's Division took no advantage of its position. How near to, and yet how far from, succouring Napoleon was Grouchy! A little forethought, more energy, and a bolder initiative on Grouchy's part would have overcome the opposition of the elements, and rendered Napoleon's great stroke a success.

As an example of a defence of a river and village, the battle of Wavre was a brilliant exploit. The courage on both sides was of the highest order. Thielemann held Wavre as long as he could, and only withdrew when he saw that his opportunity would occur the moment Grouchy learned the result of Waterloo. To stay in his position, after the French had taken Bierges, would have been to court disaster, but to retreat too soon would have ruined his chances of rallying again to the attack. In the previous night's attacks, the Prussians had shown great courage and tenacity, and the French were no less courageous and determined; their movements in the darkness were carried out with surprising skill, and reflect highly on their management and control. Vandamme's repeated efforts against the bridges might have been avoided, and every available man brought across the Dyle at Limale, leaving only enough men to watch Zeppelin in and around Wavre itself.

CHAPTER VIII

GROUCHY'S RETREAT

GROUCHY first heard the news of Napoleon's defeat at half-past ten on the morning of the 19th, just as he was preparing to pursue Thielemann and push his infantry towards Brussels. The news was brought by a staff officer, riding up with the most dejected appearance. He could scarcely get his words out, and Grouchy seemed at first to believe that the fellow was mad. But at last there was no doubt about it: the French had been severely beaten. What was Grouchy to do? Should he continue his own operations, as if nothing had happened, and keep his men in ignorance, whereby he might yet cover Napoleon's retreat? Or should he retreat himself before he was hemmed in?

At first he thought of marching against Blucher's rear, but very little reflection showed him that Thielemann would in the meantime attack *his* rear, and his 30,000 men would be

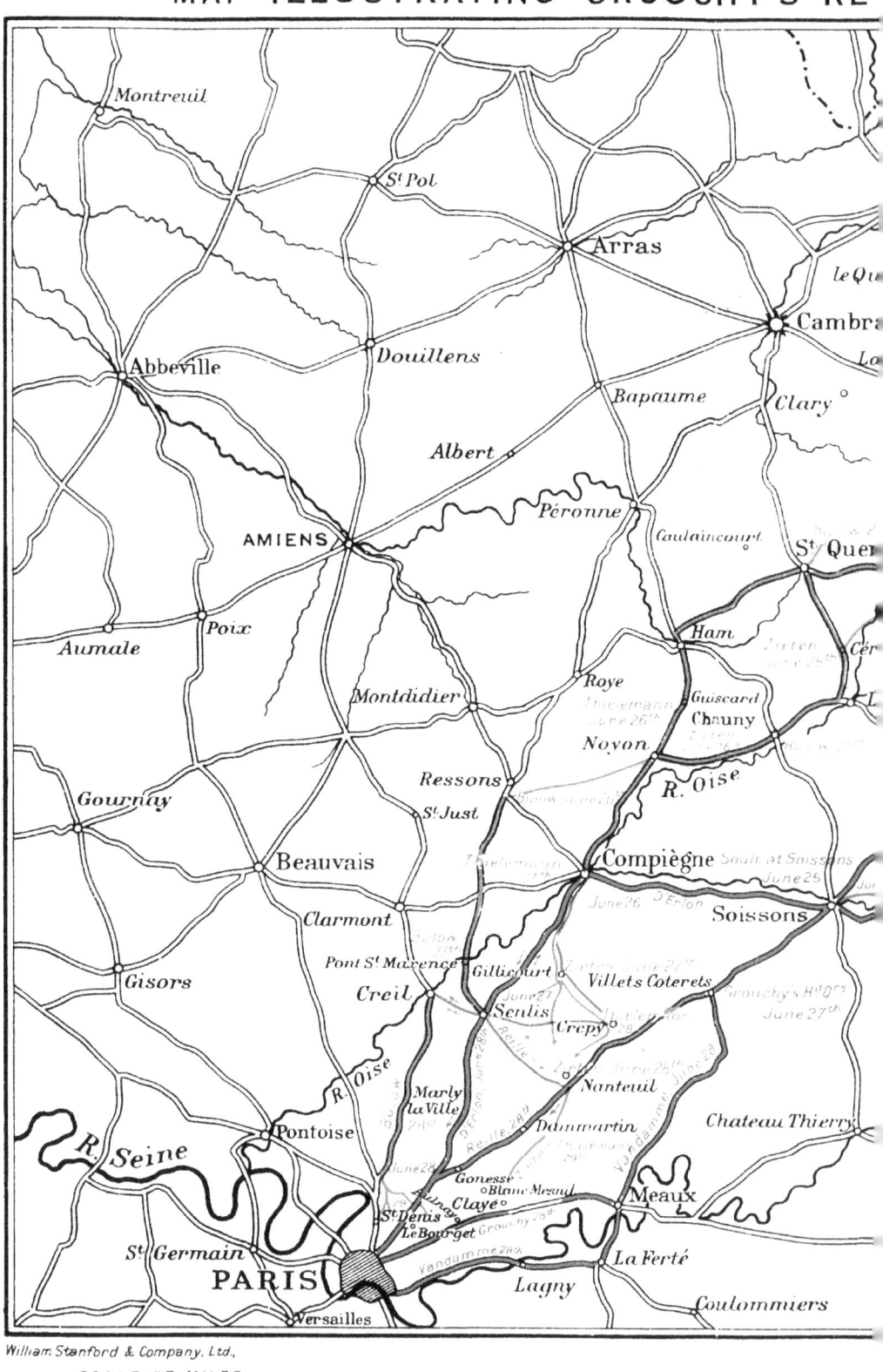

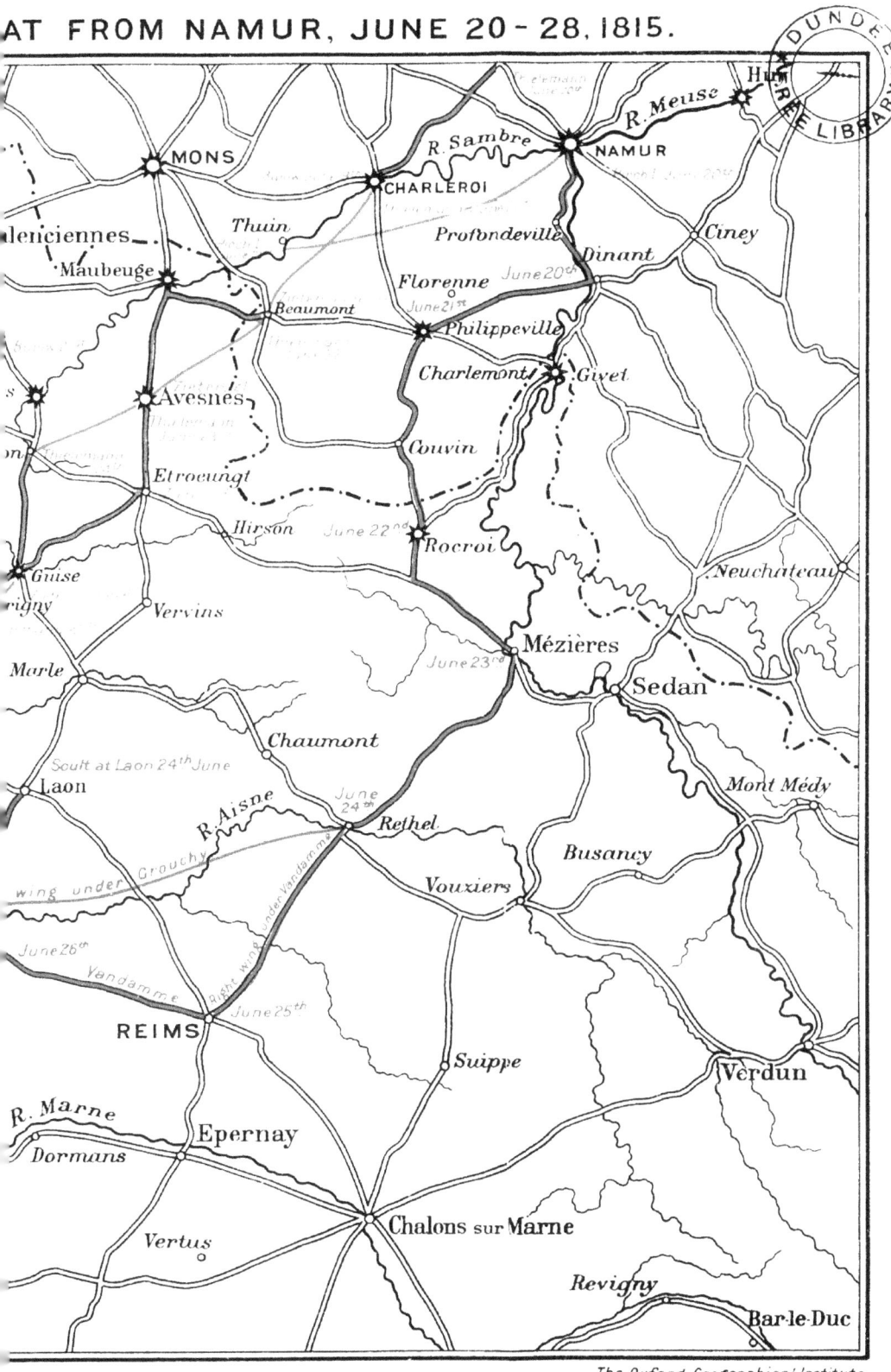

AT FROM NAMUR, JUNE 20-28, 1815.

French Retreat

caught between two forces. Then Vandamme, always impetuous and for action, proposed that they should march straight on Brussels, set free the French prisoners there, and retire by Enghien and Ath to Lille. This was a daring but futile plan.

Of what use would such a movement have been, even had it been successfully carried out? To march boldly completely round the rear of the allied armies, liberate a few prisoners, and then march off in the opposite direction, would have been to waste the only formed body left of all Napoleon's army. And what would Thielemann do in the meantime? There was now no hope of winning over Brussels or the Dutch-Belgians, otherwise there would have been some weight in Vandamme's extraordinary proposal. But Grouchy counselled otherwise. He knew that he already ran the risk of being attacked in flank, most probably in rear, by a portion of Blucher's army, while Thielemann would certainly advance again as soon as the retreat began. He therefore decided to retreat on Namur, where he would act further according to circumstances. It was useless as well as dangerous to direct his retreat towards the line taken by the remnants of Napoleon's host, where all would be confusion; it was better by far to retreat on his own line and endeavour to preserve his troops intact as long as possible. At Namur, he might do great things yet; for Namur had not, like Charleroi, witnessed first the triumph and then the downfall of Napoleon's last plans.

Even at this moment, Grouchy was already in danger of being attacked in rear. For Pirch I. had received orders on the night of the 18th to march towards Namur with his Corps (the Second) and cut off Grouchy from the Sambre; and by the time that Grouchy heard of the rout, he had reached Mellery, on the Tilly-Mont St Guibert road, and 8 miles in Grouchy's rear. But his troops were exhausted, and his Divisions scattered—the Sixth, Seventh, Eighth Divisions, twenty-four squadrons of his reserve cavalry, and the reserve artillery, were with him; but the Fifth Division and the rest of his cavalry were pursuing the French on the Charleroi road. So Pirch ordered a halt at Mellery.

Blucher's main body was pursuing the French by Charleroi in the direction of Avesnes and Laon. The cavalry of the First and Fourth Corps, also twelve squadrons belonging to the Second Corps, were at this time following up the fugitives between Frasnes and Gosselies, while the Prussian infantry followed as rapidly as their exhaustion would allow. Bulow's Corps had pursued over-night as far as Genappe, where it bivouacked, and then resumed its march at daybreak, sending out cavalry—the 8th Prussian Hussars, followed by two other regiments—to watch Grouchy's movements on the left. The Fourth Corps was leading the Prussian main body in the pursuit. The First Corps followed, and likewise sent out cavalry to watch the left flank for signs of Grouchy.

Meanwhile, Grouchy began his retreat. His troops had reached the line La Bavette-Rosieren, in their pursuit of Thielemann, and now Excelmans' Cavalry was sent off with orders to make all speed to Namur and secure the bridges over the Sambre at that place. Excelmans reached Namur at 4.30 P.M., a little more than five hours to cover 30 miles by devious lanes and byways in a terrible condition after the rains.

Gérard's Corps, preceded by the Seventh Cavalry Division (six squadrons under Vallin, who had taken Maurin's place), re-crossed the Dyle by the bridge at Limale, and moved by a narrow lane to the main Namur-Brussels road. Vandamme's Corps withdrew from La Bavette, and marched through Wavre, Dion-le-Mont, Chaumont, Tourinnes, Sart à Walhain, Grand

Leez, St. Denis to Temploux on the Namur-Nivelles road, where it arrived at 11 P.M. and there bivouacked. Gérard's Corps had reached Temploux an hour earlier.

Pajol, in command of the rear-guard, which was composed of the Fourth Cavalry Division—twelve squadrons, under Baron Soult—and Teste's Infantry Division, demonstrated against Thielemann to keep him occupied until Wavre had been cleared, and then retreated by Corbaix, Walhain, Sauvenière, to Gembloux, where he bivouacked for the night.

As has been seen, Pirch was at Mellery with the Second Corps during the 19th from 11 A.M.; but he did not wish to risk attacking Grouchy without news of Thielemann. Grouchy's army was still in good order and capable of stout fighting, but Pirch might have assisted the general situation by at least threatening Gérard's right flank as he retreated. It is not likely that Grouchy would have checked his retreat on Namur, even if Pirch had shown himself, but Gérard would have been obliged to face round, and might possibly have been cut off; or if Grouchy had halted to confront Pirch, Thielemann would have had a good opportunity to attack him in flank.

Thielemann only heard of the French retreat

towards 6 P.M. on the 19th, and his intelligence came through General Borcke, who discovered Grouchy's movement, from St Lambert. Pajol had a rear-guard still in front of Thielemann, and as the latter's troops were tired with their recent exertions, the Prussians postponed their pursuit until the next day, the 20th, when Borcke was ordered to march at daybreak with the Ninth Division from St Lambert, across the Dyle, and towards Namur.

At daybreak on the 20th, Grouchy's rear-guard left Gembloux and marched on Namur by St Denis and La Falize. His infantry left Temploux about 9 A.M. Gérard's Corps was intended to lead, Vandamme's Corps covering the retreat of the Fourth, but Vandamme upset the arrangements by betaking himself over-night to Namur, leaving no instructions behind him for his Divisional generals. Consequently, the Divisions of the Third Corps moved off by themselves, early in the morning, and Gérard's Corps, which was carrying the wounded with it, was left uncovered. A short distance beyond Temploux, the column was attacked by Prussian cavalry which had been sent off in pursuit by Thielemann at daybreak that morning. And at the same time, more cavalry were seen coming against the rear, along the Nivelles-Namur road.

This was the cavalry heading Pirch's Corps which had marched from Mellery to Sombreffe. Gérard's column had now stumbled on Vandamme's rear-guard, posted 3 miles outside Namur; and Vandamme himself coming out from Namur, Grouchy ordered him to clear the road for the Fourth Corps, and cover its march with his rear-guard.

Thielemann's Cavalry, accompanied by a battery of horse artillery, had come on at a great pace, and were almost too exhausted to attack the French with any vigour; but they managed to drive back the enemy's cavalry and capture three guns. Further attack on the French rear-guard was left to Pirch's Corps, which was now hurrying up.

The French retreated through Namur, after being well treated by the inhabitants (who supplied them with food, transport, and boats), and leaving Teste's Division with eight guns in defence of the town against Pirch's Corps. The remainder of Grouchy's army crossed the Sambre by the Namur bridge and marched on Dinant by the valley of the Meuse.

In Namur, Teste made a brilliant defence. The town was fortified, but the works were out-of-date and dilapidated; and there was no time to improve the local resources. Teste's men only numbered 2,000, with eight guns, and Pirch's Corps was some 20,000 strong. All the wounded, the baggage, and the transport had been sent across the Sambre, and the bridge barricaded.

Pirch had suffered severely in his attack on Vandamme's rear-guard outside Namur, losing over 1,200 men. The French had beaten back his three assaulting columns, and withdrawn into the town without letting the Prussian cavalry cut them off. Consequently Pirch was in no mind for a costly assault on Namur while Teste's Division held the place; and he knew that Teste would not hold his position longer than was absolutely necessary for Grouchy with the main body to gain a safe distance. He contented himself with holding the enemy's attention in front, while he despatched the main body of the Seventh Division to threaten the retreat over the Sambre. But as soon as the main portion of Grouchy's army had cleared the river, Teste began to make his own preparations for retreat. He ordered a sortie to be made against the Prussians on the north, to gain time and to divert their attention from the bridge; and when all was ready, he withdrew his troops rapidly in single file across the parapets of the barricaded bridge, setting fire to a heap of faggots and lumber piled up against the enemy's end. The guns had to be left behind.

It was nightfall now—that is to say, towards 9 P.M.—when Teste's Division filed across the bridge. The Prussians entered on the north, but their way was barred by obstacles, and they were too late to prevent the last men from escaping over the river. Their pursuit was checked by the burning barricades, which had to be put out before the bridge could be used; and the troops were halted in the town for the night, only a few cavalry being pushed across the river on the road to Dinant, ready for pursuit next day.

Teste continued his retreat unharmed, and reached Dinant at daybreak next day, the 21st. Grouchy's main body had arrived there overnight, and the whole force proceeded to Phillippeville on the 21st. Pirch spent the night at Namur with his Corps; Thielemann's cavalry at Temploux, his infantry at Gembloux.

Between Namur and Dinant, Grouchy had barricaded every narrow passage, and placed obstacles at intervals on the roads; and in this way hindered the chances of Prussian pursuit, and gaining time for himself.

The scattered remnants of Napoleon's army were fleeing along the roads from Charleroi towards Avesnes, Laon, and Phillippeville. Grouchy therefore designed his retreat so as to bring his army clear of pursuit as quickly as possible, and to work his way towards the fragments which were with difficulty being collected round Laon by Soult, Reille, and others. He hoped to reach Paris before the allied armies, in time to organise a defence, or perhaps to effect a junction with the army of the Alps under Suchet and with Lecourbe. Napoleon himself had given up the plan of rallying his routed army under Grouchy's still formidable force, and had ridden in haste to Paris, where his position was already precarious.

On the 21st, Grouchy marched from Dinant to Phillippeville, but Pirch I. did not pursue. His Corps was required elsewhere, to blockade some of the fortresses which barred the line of advance of Blucher's army. Grouchy might have retired through Givet and down the valley of the Meuse, instead of risking the more dangerous road to Phillippeville. But his aim was to draw near to any body of troops which were left from Napoleon's army, and to avoid marching down the narrow defile of the Meuse valley where he would be liable to an attack in flank or in rear, under great disadvantages. Zieten was at Beaumont on 20th June, 12 miles from Phillippeville, but he had marched at daybreak on the 21st. Pirch, marching to Thuin on the 21st, was moving parallel to Grouchy, but the latter's march was not hindered.

Four French fortresses barred Blucher's advance—Landrécies, Maubeuge, Avesnes and Rocroi. It was necessary to reduce these before any further advance on Paris was made; hence Grouchy was able to retreat unmolested for the greater part of his movement. On the 22nd he reached Rocroi; and Mezières on the 23rd. His force constituted an important menace to the left flank of the Prussian army; and Blucher was thus obliged to detach several parties of cavalry to watch the French movements.

Zieten took Avesnes on the 21st, and Grouchy's march from Phillippeville to Rocroi was in danger; but his strength was not accurately known at the Prussian headquarters, and Blucher was anxious to push on to Paris. The fall of Paris was expected to put an end to the French resistance. The capture of Avesnes relieved Blucher of the danger which threatened his army if he advanced, and it also gave him an advanced depôt for his supplies.

On the 22nd, Soult was at Laon endeavouring

to collect the remnants of Napoleon's army. He succeeded in gathering some 3,000 fugitives, mostly of Reille's Corps and d'Erlon's, and with these he hoped to join Grouchy. Urgent messages from Paris implored Grouchy to unite all the forces he could find and oppose the advance of the allies. This was easier said than done, for it was now a race between Blucher and Grouchy. Grouchy had to take a long detour to avoid being cut off; while the Prussians could advance direct on Paris, leaving detachments to watch the fortresses which might prove dangerous in the rear, and keeping close observation on the left flank on Grouchy's operations. Those fortresses which had not been taken by Zieten and Bulow were blockaded by Pirch, and nearly all of them—at least all those which menaced the advance—being garrisoned by ill-spirited and disheartened troops, and capable of little resistance, were compelled to surrender. But Blucher was careful to take no risks, and systematically he cleared the way for his advance. The shorter line by which he marched ensured his reaching Paris before Grouchy, if only with one Corps. Retreating troops move quickly, but the Prussians proved themselves capable of some wonderful forced marches.

For the French it was a time when the Napoleon of former days would have revived the broken fortunes of his country, and rallied every soldier for the protection of Paris. He would have brought up all the troops in the West, from the Pyrenees, and from the Alps; and he would have led a new army of 100,000 or 150,000 men against Blucher. The old strategy of 1814 would have been repeated, and many a loss suffered by the allies before they could bring all their six armies to converge on Paris. But now there was no Napoleon to fill the vacancy. The Emperor was defeated in Paris as well as at Mont St Jean. He had no party, no power; Frenchmen were wearied and sickened by the disasters he had brought on their country through his insatiable ambition. Grouchy alone showed power and resolution; yet he only led his forces in retreat. Could he still save the country?

The 23rd was a day of comparative rest for the Prussian army. Blucher was anxious to draw in his Corps for his advance on Paris. Thielemann moved from Beaumont to Avesnes. On the 24th the advance was resumed. The Prussian army was to march in two columns. On the left, nearer Grouchy, Zieten's and Thielemann's Corps were to march by the valley of the Oise on Compiègne, keeping a sharp watch for Grouchy. On the right, Bulow's Corps, the Fourth, was to march by St Quentin, Ham, Roye, to Pont St Maxence.

On the 24th Zieten took Guise without firing a shot, and thus secured another important point, to serve as a depôt, and as a refuge for wounded. The First Corps halted for the night in the town, sending out its cavalry as far as La Fère and Marle. Thielemann marched from Avesnes to Nouvion, and threw out scouts to Hirson and Vervins. Bulow reached the neighbourhood of St Quentin.

Grouchy, on the 24th, marched from Mezières to Réthel; Soult, from Laon to Soissons. The Prussians were observed to be gaining.

On the 25th Zieten moved from Guise to Cérisy, with cavalry towards La Fère. Thielemann marched from Nouvion to Origny; Bulow, from St Quentin to Chauny.

Grouchy, finding Soult had retreated from Laon, changed his direction, and hastened with part of his forces along the valley of the Aisne to Soissons, while Vandamme, with the remains of the Third and Fourth Corps, marched to Reims, where he arrived on the 25th.

Blucher, learning from the reports of the advanced cavalry of Soult's retreat from Laon, now directed his troops to seize the passages of the Oise, cross the river, and cut off both Grouchy and Soult between Soissons and the capital. It was a race for the bridges of the Oise, and for Crepy and Senlis.

So anxious was the Prussian Commander-in-Chief, that at midnight on the 25th-26th, he ordered Zieten to make a forced march with his advanced guard on Compiègne. A squadron of Hussars managed to reach that place at midnight on the 26th-27th, and found that a large body of French were expected there at any moment from Soissons. The remainder of Zieten's advanced guard could get no further than Noyon that night, while the main body of his Corps bivouacked at Chauny. They were too exhausted to go further that day. Thielemann, however, marched from Origny to Guiscard, 20 miles as the crow flies; and Bulow from Ham to Ressons, 25 miles.

The French, in the meantime, were also hurrying to the Oise. Grouchy had taken over the command of Soult's motley force, and d'Erlon was sent forward with about 4,000 men to reach Compiègne before the Prussians if possible, and secure the bridge there. Vandamme was hurrying from Reims towards Soissons with the Third and Fourth Corps.

At 4.30 A.M. on the 27th, Zieten's advanced guard, consisting of a Division, marching during the night, reached Compiègne, and Jagow, in command, immediately took steps for its defence. Half an hour later the head of d'Erlon's troops appeared on the Soissons road! This was indeed a narrow margin for success.

D'Erlon at once attacked, but a battery of Prussian horse artillery, posted on the road, opened such a heavy fire on his columns that the men gave way, and took refuge in a wood. From thence a sharp fire was kept up by the French skirmishers, and four guns were brought up to cope with the Prussian artillery; but these were soon silenced, and d'Erlon ordered the retreat, finding that he could no longer gain the bridge over the Oise, or delay the Prussian advance. As soon as he retreated, a regiment of Hussars was sent in pursuit, but Jagow's men were too tired by their long forced march to follow up, and d'Erlon's Corps was allowed to gain much time. Zieten with his main body reached Compiègne at mid-day; and found Blucher already there. Zieten was then ordered to send the Second Division (this division had relieved the Third, under Jagow, as advanced guard) towards Villets Coterets to cut off any force which might be retreating from Soissons on Paris; also to send his reserve cavalry and artillery to Gillicourt.

Just as Zieten's troops reached Gillicourt, d'Erlon's rear-guard left that place, and followed d'Erlon to Crepy. From Crepy, however, the French were again driven out by the Prussian cavalry, and d'Erlon retreated westwards towards Senlis, hoping to gain the bridge at Creil. Zieten's Fourth Division with his cavalry and artillery bivouacked at Gillicourt; his Second Division near Villets Coterets.

Bulow, in the meantime, was hastening down from Ressons to seize the bridges at Pont St Maxence and Creil; and his advanced guard was ordered to detach a "flying column" to secure the passages. Accordingly, Sydow took a squadron of Hussars and a company of infantry, and marched with all speed to Creil, the infantry being carried in carts. Just as the Prussians reached the bridge, part of d'Erlon's advanced cavalry was observed making for the same place from the opposite side. Sydow attacked with his squadron and drove back the French; and on the arrival of the rest of Bulow's advanced guard, a regiment of infantry was left to hold Creil, while a regiment of cavalry pushed on to Senlis, where it was expected to find d'Erlon. But on reaching that village, it was found to be unoccupied, and the Prussians halted there. At nightfall, however, Kellermann, leading d'Erlon's column, came up from Crepy with a brigade of heavy cavalry, and immediately charged down on the Prussians. The latter were unprepared, and were speedily routed. They fled back to Pont St Maxence, and Kellermann fell back on d'Erlon's infantry. Sydow now came up with the rest of Bulow's advanced guard, expecting to find Senlis already occupied by Prussians, but he was astonished by their absence. However, he occupied Senlis at 10 P.M. When d'Erlon approached, he was met with a heavy fire from the Prussian sharpshooters, who had loop-holed the nearest houses and taken shelter behind walls. Finding Senlis too strongly held, d'Erlon withdrew, and made his way towards Gonesse, while Reille took part of his force to Nanteuil. Night put an end to pursuit.

Thus at the close of the 27th, all the bridges over the Oise were in Blucher's hands, and there seemed every prospect of Grouchy's forces being cut off from Paris. The French had now three separate columns in retreat, and there was a great danger of two of these being cut off.

On the 28th, long before dawn, the Second Division of Zieten's Corps approached Villets Coterets, where Grouchy had his headquarters.

The Prussians, hearing that the place was not strongly held, resolved to carry it by surprise; but Grouchy had 9,000 men posted on the road to Nanteuil, and these attacked and drove back the Prussians. Suddenly, however, a panic seized the greater part of the French troops, who, seeing a movement of Prussian troops towards Crepy, thought that their retreat was being cut off, and they fled in a body down the road towards Meaux. Thus Villets Coterets fell into the hands of the Prussians.

Vandamme, after restoring some order among the fugitives, led them, the remains of the Third and Fourth Corps, scarcely 8,000 men, by Meaux, La Ferté, and Lagny to Paris.

Zieten pushed on to Nanteuil on the 28th, where Reille's rear-guard was found and driven out. Reille was retreating on Gonesse, to effect a junction with d'Erlon, who was falling back from Senlis. Bulow was marching rapidly on St Denis, and had reached Marly la Ville by the evening of the 28th, threatening to cut off Reille and d'Erlon. Thielemann hastened from Compiègne and reached Crepy that night.

On the 29th Blucher's Corps closed in, and by nightfall they occupied the following positions:—Bulow's Corps at Le Bourget and St Denis; Thielemann's Corps at Dammartin; Zieten's at

Blanc Mesnil and Aulnay. Grouchy's forces had entered Paris, having lost 4,000 men and 16 guns in the numerous skirmishes along the Oise. But they had won the race, and their retreat must be considered as a skilful operation. It had little actual effect on the advance of the allies, but Grouchy, who had so slurred his reputation in the great operations entrusted to him by Napoleon, in his retreat somewhat retrieved his character as a general.

CHAPTER IX

NOTES AND COMMENTS

1. CHAPTER II.—The proportion of cavalry to infantry in Grouchy's force was large (more than one to five), but not excessive. He was given a task in which cavalry must play the chief part. At the close of such a battle as Ligny, the infantry on both sides must be more or less exhausted, and it becomes the duty of the cavalry to pursue the retreating enemy. Cavalry alone, however, will effect little, if the enemy takes to rear-guard positions; it must be supported or accompanied by artillery and infantry. It must be remembered that, of the two sides, the vanquished are the more exhausted, and the greater the enemy's anxiety to draw his troops clear of pursuit, the closer that pursuit must be. The French cavalry at Ligny, except Milhaud's Cuirassiers, had had little to do.

The proportion of cavalry to infantry in an army cannot be laid down by any hard-and-fast rule. Prince Kraft wrote after 1870: "The duties of the cavalry are so comprehensive and so important, especially at the first moment of a war, that we cannot have too many cavalry ready for service." But he was speaking of Germany. Continental armies require a far larger number of cavalry than our own; and not only for the reason that their other arms are so much more numerous than ours. The advance of modern armies is covered by a most numerous cavalry, sent out, as were the German cavalry in 1870, miles ahead, as a screen, and for the purpose of reconnaissance, or to harass the enemy's concentration and cut his communications.

2. *The French Corps in* 1815.—The French Corps in the 1815 Campaign were more independent than the Prussian Corps—that is to say, each corps, except Lobau's, was provided with sufficient cavalry and artillery to enable it to act by itself. Each corps had a Light Cavalry Division; but in Grouchy's force, the Cavalry Division (Domon's) belonging to Vandamme's Corps, with its horse battery, had been detached to the left wing. Gérard's Corps had its complete parts, but the Seventh Cavalry Division attached to it numbered only 758 men; little more than a modern regiment. The Reserve Cavalry Division, under Jacquinot, also attached to Gérard's Corps, numbered 1608 men, so that the two together would only make a modern brigade. In artillery, the corps, for those days, were well provided; and each corps also had its own engineers, from 140 to 200 strong.

3. CHAPTER III. *Pursuits after a Battle.*—A general who wins a battle must make every effort to obtain the greatest possible advantages from his victory; he must closely pursue the defeated enemy with cavalry, artillery, and infantry; he must spare no one until the retreat has been turned into a rout. Of the two sides, the vanquished are the more exhausted; and the effects of defeat are so demoralising that, when followed by pursuit, every vestige of organisation or power of resisting vanishes. Men whose backs are turned on a victorious enemy who is treading on their heels, harassing their flanks, and cutting them down or capturing them by thousands, will think of nothing but their personal safety. The more time that is left to the retreating force, the more rear-guard positions it will be able to take up, and every rear-guard action gives time for the retreat to be carried further and in greater security. A timid pursuit is almost worse than none. Every nerve must be strained to make the most of the situation.

Yet, in history, how many instances are there in which pursuits have been carried out? What are the reasons which account for so many battles ending without a pursuit? There are few instances, indeed, where it has been possible for the victor to follow up his victory as is advised in the books. To mention the most noted cases:—The pursuit of the French after Waterloo; the pursuit after Jena; the cavalry advance on Cairo after Tel-el-Kebir; and, most recently, the battles of the Yalu and at Telissu, in the Russo-Japanese War. But how easy it is to recall cases where pursuit has not followed the victory:—Wagram, Friedland, Vittoria, Cannae; Malplaquet, Albuera, Spicheren, Bull Run, and the case treated in this volume, among scores of others.

Many Generals have failed to take the opportunity when it was offered; Hannibal himself was one of them. But in most of the cases there have been strong reasons for the hesitation in pursuing. After a long and fiercely-contested battle, both sides are exhausted; and there may be no fresh troops at hand to carry out the pursuit. There may be heavy rains, making the road impassable; there may be a lack of mounted troops. Most of Wellington's victories in the Peninsular War were so dearly bought that his troops were far too exhausted themselves to think of pursuing the enemy. After Malplaquet Marlborough's army was in no condition to follow up the victory, and the French were able to retreat in fair order and unmolested. After Spicheren, the Prussians were too exhausted to pursue, and the French withdrew in security. But after Ligny Napoleon should have pursued, at least at daybreak on the 17th. It has been shown that he had a strong force of cavalry, as well as Lobau's Corps, available for the pursuit, and with these he could have driven Thielemann from Sombreffe. His cavalry would have threatened the Prussian flanks and rear, while Lobau's infantry would have attacked in front. During the night it was perhaps unwise and unsafe to pursue, owing to Thielemann's firm front, and to the enormous risks of a pursuit by night. No one knew better than Napoleon the value of pressing hard on a vanquished foe, and it is impossible to explain why he spent the morning of the 17th in trivialities. A day later, and he himself realised the position of a defeated general closely and mercilessly pursued by the victors.

Grouchy cannot be blamed for failing to pursue the Prussians on the night of the 16th. He was directly under the Emperor's orders, and he only received his independent command on the morning of the 17th. At 11 P.M., on the night of the 16th, he had been ordered to send Pajol and Excelmans in pursuit of the Prussians at daybreak, but no direction was given to him. And when it was found that Thielemann's men still held Sombreffe, the cavalry took no further action that night.

Blucher, on the 18th, found it possible to pursue the French with the utmost vigour by night; but there was this difference between the two cases—the French were totally defeated in battle, and demoralised, while the Prussians, at Ligny, were only partially defeated, and their left wing was firm and unbeaten.

It was on the 17th that Grouchy's mistakes began, after he had received his new command from Napoleon, at 11 A.M.

4. CHAPTER IV.—It is astonishing that the outposts of Grouchy's force in front of Sombreffe should have heard nothing, or reported nothing, of Thielemann's withdrawal, which began at 2 A.M., and continued until 4 A.M., when the rear-guard left the village. Throughout the night, the opposing sentries were within earshot; and if they were awake they could not have helped hearing the commotion which must be caused by the movement of so large a body of troops by night, however great the precautions may be. True, it was a wet night; rain was falling heavily, but not too heavily to drown the noise of the retreat. Even a perfectly-planned and well-executed attack by night, with all the signs pre-determined, and each movement marked beforehand, cannot be kept absolutely quiet; there is always a stumbling, a cry of pain from a sprained ankle or

broken nose, a curse from the darkness, often a rifle accidentally discharged; but in a retreat hastily decided on, how much greater will the noise be! The shouting of orders which cannot be conveyed by signs or signals on the spur of the moment, the noise of the heavy waggons, the yells of the drivers, and the cracking of whips! In those days the outpost positions would be scarcely two hundred yards apart on such an occasion; very different to modern conditions, which would make it impossible for two forces to remain in the same positions, relative to one another, as Thielemann's and Grouchy's on that night.

5. CHAPTER IV.—Excelmans lacked the true instinct of a cavalry leader. When he found Thielemann at Gembloux, at 9.30 A.M. on the 17th, the first step we should expect him to take would be to send back immediate word to Grouchy; then he would act according to his instructions, or as his own notions prompted. In the present circumstances, he would have taken steps to harass the enemy, deceive him as to his real numbers, threaten his line of retreat, and force him to march off again, and so spoil his rest and increase the fatigue of his troops, who would soon become too tired either to march or fight, when their retreat would have rapidly become a headlong rout; or to detain him in uncertainty until the infantry arrived. Certainly, entire inactivity was wrong in such a case. Every hour of rest allowed to Thielemann meant that his troops would be able to march more rapidly when they took the road again. If Thielemann had seen a few squadrons threatening his retreat, a few showing themselves on his flanks, without knowing the real strength of the force overtaking him, it is not conceivable that he would have waited to be attacked by overwhelming numbers.

6. CHAPTER IV.—It must have disconcerted Napoleon to hear Grouchy expostulating as to the orders which he had just given him. The Napoleon of earlier days would have

dealt with a heavy hand on the man who dared discuss his orders. No doubt Grouchy felt very strongly on the subject, and his views may very well have been sound—in fact, they were sound up to a certain point; but it is never a soldier's duty to discuss or argue about his orders. The story of Grouchy's insubordination—for insubordination it certainly was—would be difficult to credit, but that some of the best authorities on the campaign give it in their works; and Grouchy himself, in his "Relation Succincte," openly admits that he made no attempt, in his conversation with the Emperor, to conceal his misgivings.

7. CHAPTER IV.—The mismanagement of the places of assembly and the times of starting the march of different bodies of troops which have to take the same road, leads to miserable confusion. In the present case, there were two Corps d'Armée, Gérard's and Vandamme's, which were required to march from Ligny and St Amand La Haye respectively, to Point-du-Jour by one and the same road. It seems obvious that, time being important, and considering the positions of the two Corps, Gérard's Corps should be marched off first, while Vandamme's should follow as soon as it was ready. But Grouchy, for no reason which can be found, ordered Vandamme to take the lead. Gérard had to wait over one hour while Vandamme's Corps passed him.

It is not an easy matter to arrange, in a case of this kind, that the front corps should be clear by the time that the head of the corps in rear comes up; but Gérard's Corps was sufficiently far ahead of Vandamme's to allow plenty of time for his men to get on their way before the latter approached, and, at all events, it would have been better to halt Vandamme, while Gérard moved well on the road, than to keep Gérard waiting while Vandamme passed him.

8. CHAPTER IV.—Vandamme's march on Gembloux was extremely slow. He left his bivouac at 12 noon, and

arrived at Point-du-Jour, less than 4 miles off, at 3 P.M., and at Gembloux, another 5 miles, at 7 P.M. The roads, it must be remembered, were in a deplorable condition, and the rain was falling steadily; but the rate of marching, when compared with the rate of the Prussians over the same road, in only slightly better condition of surface, and with the rate in Grouchy's subsequent retreat, also in heavy weather, is extraordinarily slow. The guns were moved with great difficulty, and it must be supposed that infantry in large numbers were used to drag them along, but there were still horses to be used, and the Prussians had moved all their guns and waggons successfully. The state of the weather has always been urged in extenuation of Grouchy's slowness in this campaign, but it has been laboured too much. It certainly was a very heavy factor against him, but not so overpowering as is alleged.

9. CHAPTER IV.—Grouchy wasted valuable time in bivouacking at Gembloux, when there were still two hours of daylight left. His men must have been tired with their exertions through the mud; but they had not made extraordinary efforts. French soldiers had proved themselves capable of greater things in other days, and under other commanders. Had they even pushed on to Sauvenière that night, they would have arrived early enough to allow themselves some six or eight hours' rest; or even longer if the cavalry were used with skill. The difficulties of this particular march are often exaggerated; compare it with the marching of the same men two days later, over the same roads, and after continuous fighting for several hours; compare it, too, with some of the marches in the Peninsula, a few years before!

10. CHAPTER IV.—Grouchy's despatch from Gembloux on the night of the 17th to the Emperor cannot be read without a feeling of surprise at his words. In the first place, he says, "My cavalry is at Sauvenière." Now, Napoleon would

naturally infer that Pajol's cavalry were included; or that all the cavalry were probably together. It was misleading to say that his "cavalry was at Sauvenière." Secondly, "They (the Prussians) were still here at ten o'clock this morning." The Emperor would at once conclude that the enemy had left soon after ten o'clock; he certainly would suppose that Grouchy would have found out if they had remained there later. Actually, the Prussians left at 2 P.M., four hours later. Thirdly, "He (Blucher) has not passed by Gembloux." Napoleon would suppose (since Grouchy had been instructed to keep touch with the left wing) that traces of Blucher and his main body had been searched for between the line of Grouchy's march and the main French army. On these three essential points, the information given in the despatch was decidedly misleading. Some other details were inaccurate, but they were reasonable convictions, as far as Grouchy's views went. Negative information in war is very often as useful and important as positive; and Grouchy would have assisted Napoleon to form his ideas if he had reported that he had discovered no signs of a Prussian retreat on Namur. He should also have made some mention of Pajol's detachment—such as "no news has been received from Pajol, who is on my right at St Denis, with a detachment of cavalry and infantry." Again, had Grouchy only accounted for 30,000 Prussians, of the whole of Blucher's army? What had become of the remainder? Where were they?

Napoleon must have found it impossible to draw inferences of any weight from this despatch; and in such a campaign as this, full and accurate intelligence was of the utmost importance.

11. CHAPTER V.—A flank march in presence of the enemy is a most difficult and dangerous operation. In the case of Blucher's movement, there was little actual danger from Grouchy, as events proved, but in face of a vigorous enemy the Prussians would have been in a perilous position.

It was possible for an active enemy to seize the bridges over the Dyle at Moustier and Ottignies, and fall upon Blucher's flank. The latter was not exposing his communications, for his real communications were with Liege; he had temporarily abandoned them when he marched on Wavre; but if attacked during his march his position would not have been by any means safe. If defeated, whither would he have fallen back? This is the chief danger of a flank march : the lack of a good, or even of any, line of retreat. As a rule, a flank march, being away from the general line of advance or retreat, has necessarily to be made on lesser roads, and the difficulty of ample movement from one to another, or of rapid deployment or change of front, becomes prodigious. Blucher, if attacked during this march, would most probably have left one corps to detain the enemy, while he, with the other three corps, resumed his march towards Wellington; for to turn back would have been as dangerous as to advance. But if his way had been barred he would have fallen back on Brussels rather than upon Louvain, as he would still have a chance of joining Wellington. If Blucher had been so attacked and defeated, Grouchy would have been able to deal a terrible, in all probability a crushing, blow on Wellington's left flank.

It is interesting, but not particularly profitable, to speculate as to what course events would have taken had Grouchy been up in time to prevent Blucher's flank march, and had checked him. Would Wellington have fallen back on Brussels with Blucher, and fought again under the city walls against Napoleon and Grouchy combined? In that case, the weight of numbers would have been very much in favour of the allies, and the great object of Napoleon's plan of campaign—to prevent the junction of the two armies— would have been thwarted. If Blucher, after being checked, had fallen back on Louvain, while Wellington was still engaged with Napoleon, it seems obvious that Grouchy's extra numbers thrown into the fight would have caused the Duke's overthrow, for it would not then have been necessary for Napoleon to detach against the Prussians; Wellington was too seriously engaged to be able to withdraw, and the defeat would have been complete. But after all, such speculation as this might be continued indefinitely; and every campaign might be discussed and argued to a hundred different conclusions by re-modelling the conditions or improvising situations. A campaign, like a chess problem, admits of more than one solution.

12. *Grouchy's Retreat.* CHAPTER VIII.—A few points concerning Grouchy's retreat may be discussed briefly. Firstly, could he have been intercepted before he reached Namur? The answer is Yes, by Pirch I. Pirch had received orders, on the night of the 18th, to cut off Grouchy from the Sambre; and he had accordingly marched towards Namur through Maransart. He reached Mellery at 11 A.M. on the 19th. At this hour, Grouchy had not begun his retreat. But Pirch's men were tired, and they were halted at Mellery. Had they pushed on another six miles to Gembloux, which they would have reached at 2 P.M., Grouchy's retreat on Namur would have been intercepted. It is true that Grouchy's force would have greatly outnumbered Pirch's, but the former would not stop to engage the Prussians at Gembloux while Thielemann pressed close on his heels. He would have been forced to make a very wide detour, and in the meantime the Prussians could have hastened on and captured Namur.

Secondly, after Namur, why was not Grouchy more closely pursued? It would have been an idle move to detach a force to follow Grouchy while the advance on Paris was of such immediate importance. At best, Grouchy could threaten the Prussian flank; but he would be more likely to endeavour to join with the remnants of Napoleon's army collected by Soult. Little harm could be done by these forces; and the contagion of defeat might have spread from Soult's fugitives and demoralised Grouchy's men. In any case, the other allied armies were approaching the frontier, and these would be able to deal with Grouchy. The important move was to march on Paris, where the populace, sickened by Napoleon's collapse, were likely to accept terms.

Thirdly, could Grouchy really hope to effect anything advantageous by his retreat on Paris? No, unless he saw a chance of persuading Napoleon to put himself at the head of his troops and the Paris garrison, and march out to repeat the strokes of 1814; but on the 22nd Napoleon had abdicated.

Fourthly, could he have effected more by marching south to rally Suchet and Lecourbe? Hardly; since overwhelming armies were approaching on that side, and the fall of Paris would render resistance in the country districts useless.

His case was really hopeless from the first. The allies in their march on Paris would ignore him, and, moving by a much more direct road, would reach the capital first. The triple line of fortresses across the line of advance of the enemy, were expected to bar his approach, but they were weakly garrisoned by ill-disciplined and raw troops, whose whole spirit was shaken by Napoleon's great defeat.

So far-reaching is the effect of a defeat as great as Waterloo that armies, districts, even capitals, miles from the real theatre of war, possibly in other countries, seem to crumble to dust before the conqueror; but no fall from might and power has ever been so great as Napoleon's.

INDEX

AISEMONT, village of, 68, 100, 103
Aisne river, 13, 146
Aix-la-Chapelle, 44
Allies, earlier operations of the, 1-50
Alten, General, Third British Division, 34, 42
Anthing, General, Dutch-Belgians, 34, 39
Antwerp, 8
Artillery, Prussian, 54
Asserre, 10
Ath, 7-9, 34, 35
Aulnay, 151
Avesnes, 13-15, 135, 142, 143, 145, 146

BACHELU, General, Infantry Division (French), 18, 33, 39, 42
Balâtre, 62, 80
Basle, 4
Basse Wavre, 109-114, 117, 118, 123, 126
Baudeset, 70
Beaumont, 4, 7, 15, 142, 145
Berthézène, Colonel, Eleventh Division, Third French Corps, 57
Berton, General, Brigade of French Dragoons, 81, 82
Bianchi, General (Austrians), 4
Bierges, mill of, 111, 117-119, 122, 126, 127
———, village of, 68, 103, 111, 113, 118, 120, 124, 126-129
Binche, 33
Blanc Mesnil, 151
Blucher, General, 4, 71, 83, 133; his army in Belgium, 9, 10; at Sombreffe, 21, 22, 25, 26; his reasons for concentrating at Ligny, 35-37, 43-47; interview with Wellington at Bussy, 40; defeated by Napoleon at Ligny, 73, 78; his retreat, 84, 90, 92; makes for Brussels, 94; marches towards Mont St Jean, 100-107; ordered to defend Wavre, 108; pursues French by Charleroi, 135; race for Paris between Grouchy and, 143-146, 151; at Compiègne, 148; captures bridges over the Oise, 150
Bonne Espérance, 9
Bonnemain, General, 88, 89, 92
Borcke, General, Ninth Division, Third Prussian Corps, 52, 70, 109-111, 113, 115, 130, 131, 138
Bornstaedt, Major, 114
Borstel, General, 90
Bourmont, General de, 61
Braine, l'Alleud, 102
Braine-le-Comte, 8, 34, 35, 39
Brunswick, Duke of, 39, 42
Brussels, Napoleon resolves to attack, 6, 7
Bry, 73, 74
Bulow, General, Fourth Corps, 10, 66, 69, 78, 102; Gneisenau's instructions—a serious delay, 22-24; too late for Ligny, 45, 46; at Baudeset, 70; without news, 71; at Dion-le-Mont, 100, 103; reaches St Lambert, 105, 117; pursues French to Genappe, 136; marches to St Quentin, 146; Ressons, 147; Senlis, 149, 150; and Marly la Ville, 151
Bussy, mill of, 40
Bylandt, General, First Brigade, Dutch-Belgians, 33, 39

CAVALRY, Prussian, 54
Cérisy, 146
Chambre, 128

Chapelle St Lambert, 103, 105, 106, 109, 117
Charlemont, 83
Charleroi, 7, 9, 17, 25, 27, 28, 33, 36, 37, 141
Chassé, General, 34
Chastel, Colonel, Tenth Division, Second Cavalry Corps (French), 59
Châtelet, 27, 30, 37
Châtelineau, 30
Chaumont, 136
Chauny, 146, 147
Chimay, 14
Ciney, 10
Clinton, General, Second British Division, 34, 35, 39
Colville, General, Fourth British Division, 34, 35
Compiègne, 146-148, 151
Condé, 7, 8
Cooke, General, First British Division, 34, 35, 42
Corbaix, 71, 72, 94, 98, 137
Courcelles, 27
Courtrai, 8
Couture, 104, 130
Creil, 149
Crepy, 147, 149-151

DAMMARTIN, 151
Davoût, 5, 63
Dender river, 8
D'Erlon, General, First Corps (French), 12, 15, 16, 20, 21, 36, 39, 41-43, 46, 48-50, 144, 147-151
Dessaix, 63
Dinant, 9, 10, 72, 139, 141, 142
Dion-le-Mont, village of, 71, 98, 100, 103, 104, 109, 110, 115, 117, 136
Dittfurth, Major, 55, 56, 110
Domon, General, 76
Dornberg, General, 34, 35
Durutte, General, 21
Dyle river, 68, 72, 93, 96, 98-100, 104-106, 110-112, 114, 118, 122, 124, 126, 129, 136, 138

ENGHIEN, 8, 9, 34, 35, 39
Ernage, 72, 89
Excelmans, General, Second Cavalry Corps (French), 13, 56, 59, 63, 73, 75, 76, 80-90, 92, 95-98, 107, 109, 110, 115, 117, 119, 123, 136

FERDINAND, Archduke, 3
Fleurus, 10, 17, 21, 27, 29, 32, 75
Florennes, 15, 16
Fontaine l'Evêque, 28
Foy, General, 18, 38, 42
Frasnes, 8, 18, 19, 33, 35, 38-41, 135
Frimont, Marshal, 4
Frischermont, 109

GEMBLOUX, 40, 56, 66, 68-70, 81-88, 94, 95, 137, 138, 141
Genappe, 8, 41, 136
Gentinnes, 66-68, 70, 72
Gérard, General, Fourth Corps (French), 12, 15-17, 30, 36, 58, 61, 62, 64, 73, 85-87, 94, 95, 99, 107, 115, 117-119, 124, 127, 136-139
Gerpinnes, 9, 15
Ghent, 8
Gillicourt, 149
Gilly, 17, 27, 28, 30
Girard, General, 29, 41, 42, 47-49
Givet, 4, 7
Gneisenau, General, chief of Blucher's Staff, 22-24, 66, 67, 102, 106
Gonesse, 150, 151
Gosselies, 18, 27, 28, 38, 48, 135
Grammont, 8, 34, 35
Grand Leez, 92, 99, 136
Grouchy, Marshal Count, 5, 13-15, 17, 18, 30, 42, 55, 57, 62, 64, 74-76, 78, 100, 105-107, 112; summary of his Forces, 60; unfit for independent command, 63; the only man available, 65; his pursuit of the Prussians, 80-99; battle of Wavre, 115, 117, 118, 120, 123-132; his retreat after Wavre, 133-152
Guiscard, 147
Guise, 146

HABERT, General, Tenth Division, Third French Corps, 57, 116
Ham, 146, 147
Ham-sur-Heure, 15
Hannut, 10, 22-24
Hautain-le-Val, 33

INDEX

Heppignies, village of, 29
Heron, 9
Hill, Lord, 8
Hirson, 146
Hobe, General, Reserve Cavalry, Third Prussian Corps, 53, 70, 113, 119
Hologne, 10
Houssaye, quoted, 6, 7, 61, 85
Hulot, Colonel, Fourteenth Division, Fourth French Corps, 58, 118, 119, 127
Huy, 9, 10

INFANTRY, Prussian, 54

JACQUINOT, General, Reserve Cavalry, Fourth French Corps, 50, 58
Jagow, Colonel, 148
Jamioux, 15
Jerome, General, 18, 38, 42
Jumet, 18, 21, 28

KAMPFEN, Colonel, 52, 113
Kellermann, General, Third Cavalry Corps (French), 13, 39-43, 63, 150
Kleist, General, 2

LA BARAQUE, 72, 95, 97-99, 109, 115
La Bavette, 72, 103, 113, 114, 130, 136
La Bavette-Rosieren, 136
La Falize, 138
La Fère, 146
La Ferté, 151
La Haye, 102
La Huzelle, wood of, 98, 106
Lagny, 151
Lambusart, 31
Landrécies, fortress of, 143
Langres, 4
Lannes, General, 63
Laon, 4, 13, 14, 135, 142, 143, 146
Lasne, valley of the, 104, 105
Laurent, Napoleon's A.D.C., 48
Le Boquet, 81
Le Bourget, 151
Le Caillou farm-house, 99
Le Mazy, 81, 82, 84, 89, 92
Lecourbe, General, 5, 142

Ledebur, Colonel, 71, 97, 98, 104, 106, 125
Leers, 15, 18
Lefebvre-Desnouette, General, Cavalry of the Guard (French), 19, 39
Lefol, Colonel, Eighth Division, Third French Corps, 57, 117, 118
Letort, General, 31
Leuze, 8
Liège, 10, 24, 33, 90
Liers, 10
Ligny, 32, 35, 37, 38, 40, 41, 43, 44, 47, 55, 57, 62, 67, 74
Lille, 7, 12, 14
Limale, village of, 99, 100, 111, 114, 117, 119, 120, 124, 126, 132, 136
Limelette, village of, 98, 99, 112
Lobau, General, Sixth Corps (French), 13, 15-17, 36, 56, 59, 73, 76
Lobbes, village of, 9, 25
Longwy, 13
Lootz, 10
Losthin, General, 104
Lottum, Colonel Count, Reserve Cavalry, Third Prussian Corps, 53, 70, 72, 114, 128
Louvain, 81, 100, 103, 130
Luck, Colonel, Eleventh Division, Third Prussian Corps, 52, 113
Lutzow, Colonel, 28
Lyons, 5

MAESTRICHT, 83
Maladrie, hamlet of, 25, 26
Maransart, 104, 105
Marbais, 41, 47, 48, 79
Marchienne, 15, 18, 21, 26, 27
Marcinelle, 15, 28
Marle, 146
Marly la Ville, 151
Marwitz, Colonel (Prussians), 49, 50, 70, 72, 113, 126, 128-130
Masséna, General, 63
Maubeuge, fortress of, 4, 14, 15 143
Maurin, General, 107
Meaux, 151
Mellery, 66, 135, 137
Metz, 13
Meuse valley, 7, 139

INDEX

Mézières, 12, 14, 143, 146
Milhaud, General, Fourth Cavalry Corps (French), 13, 62, 63, 73
Mohnhaupt, Colonel, Reserve Artillery (Prussian), 53
Mons, 8, 25, 33, 34, 44
Mont Potriaux, 55, 56
Mont St Guibert, 66, 68, 71, 97, 100, 103, 104, 106
Mont St Jean, 44, 95, 99; Blucher marches towards, 100-107
Montigny, 26
Moustier, 93, 96, 99, 107
Muffling, 102
Murat, 63

NAMUR, 9, 10, 24, 33, 35, 83, 90, 100, 134-136, 138-141
Nancy, 4
Nanteuil, 150, 151
Napoleon, his waiting tactics and inaction, 2, 3, 36, 37, 44, 50, 76, 78; his scheme of campaign, 5, 11; resolves to attack Brussels, 6; his army for invasion of Belgium, 12; his first movements, 14; his position on 15th June, 35; his instructions to Ney, 40, 41; Ligny and after, 45, 47, 48, 73-78; Blucher's reasons, 46; Grouchy and, 64, 65, 93, 105; his orders to Grouchy, 80, 83-85, 87, 99, 117; Grouchy's despatches to, 90, 94; routed at Mont St Jean, 124; defeated at Wavre, 133; "no party, no power," 145
Neuf Sart, 97
Ney, Marshal, the "bravest of the brave," 13; in command of Left Wing, 18, 29; his cautious methods, 19, 20; Frasnes, 33, 35; interview with Napoleon, 36; hesitation about Quatre-Bras, 37-39, 42, 43, 75-77; Napoleon's instructions to, 40, 41, 47, 48; his orders to d'Erlon, 49; no news from, 75-77
Nil Perrieux, 72
Nil St Vincent, 88, 97, 98
Ninove, 8, 35
Nivelles, 9, 34, 39, 41
Nouvion, 146

Noyon, 147

OHAIN, 106
Oise river, 146, 147, 150
Orange, Prince of, commander of troops in the Netherlands, 2, 8, 34, 35, 39, 40, 42
Origny, 146, 147
Orneau, valley of the, 82
Ostend, 8
Ottenburg, village of, 130
Ottignies, 93, 99, 107
Oudenarde, 7-9

PAJOL, General, First Cavalry Corps (French), 13, 17, 26-28, 59, 60, 63, 73, 75, 76, 80-84, 87, 89, 92, 99, 115, 117-120, 127, 137, 138
Pecheux, Colonel, Twelfth Division, Fourth French Corps, 58, 127
Peronne, 4
Perponcher, General (Dutch-Belgians), 33, 34, 36, 39
Perwez, 88, 90
Philippeville, 7, 15, 141-143
Picton, General, 39, 42
Piéton stream, 28
Pirch I., General, Second Corps (Prussians), 9, 10, 32, 35, 41, 66-68, 73, 98, 100, 103, 105, 106, 135, 137, 139-144
Pirch II., General, 30-32
Piré, General, French Cavalry, 18, 29, 33, 36, 39, 41, 42
Plancenoit, 105
Point-du-Jour, 70, 85-87, 121, 126
Pont St Maxence, 146, 150
Provence, 4
Prussian Corps, Third, 52-65

QUATRE-BRAS, 7-9, 19, 20, 33, 35-45, 83; results of battle, 43

RANSART, 29
Rapp, General, 6
Reille, General, Second Corps (French), 12, 15, 18, 21, 25, 29, 36, 38-42, 142, 144, 150, 151
Reims, 146, 147
Ressons, 147, 149
Réthel, 146
Rixensart, 109, 127, 128, 131

INDEX

Rochefort, 10
Rocroi, fortress of, 14, 143
Roder, General, Reserve Cavalry (Prussian), 28, 31
Rouelx, 8
Roye, 146
Ryssel, General, Fourteenth Division (Prussians), 71, 105

SAARBRUCK, 4
Saarlouis, 4
St Achtenrode, village of, 130
St Amand, 41, 49, 74, 85
St Anne, village of, 68, 100
St Denis, 81, 89, 92, 137, 138, 151
St Géry, 93, 96
St Lambert, 117, 125, 138
St Quentin, 146
St Robert, 131
St Symphorien, 26
Sambre river, 15, 27, 28, 139, 140
Sart à Walhain, 88, 90, 92, 136
Sauvenière, village of, 88, 90, 95, 137
Saxe-Weimar, Prince Bernard of, 19, 20, 33, 35
Schwarzenberg, General (Austrian Army), 34
Seneffe, 8
Seulis, 147, 149-151
Sohr, Colonel, 71, 106
Soignies Forest, 8, 9, 93
Soissons, 146-148
Soleilmont, 30
Solre-sur-Sambre, 15
Sombreffe, 10, 18, 21, 32, 37, 41, 42, 44, 55; retreat of Thielemann's corps from, 66-79
Sossoye, 9, 10
Sottegheim, 35, 39
Soult, Marshal, 14, 16, 21, 40, 64, 80, 89, 142, 143, 146, 147
——, Baron, 60, 137
Steedman, General, 34, 39
Steinmetz, General, First Division of Zieten's Corps (Prussian), 25-29, 32-34, 39
Stengel, Colonel, 114; at Wavre, 119-121, 124, 130
Strolz, Colonel, Ninth Cavalry Division, Second Cavalry Corps (French), 59
Stulpnagel, Colonel, Twelfth Division Third Prussian Corps, 52, 109, 113; at Wavre, 119-121, 124, 126-128
Suchet, General, 5, 65, 142
Sydow, General, 149, 150

TEMPLOUX, 137, 138, 141
Teste, General, Twenty-first Division Third Prussian Corps, 59, 76, 81, 83, 96, 115, 119, 124, 127, 128, 137, 139-141
Thielemann, Lieutenant-General, Third Prussian Corps, 10, 52, 55, 56, 62, 81, 82, 87, 88, 90, 95, 100, 103, 106, 117, 119, 124-134, 136-139, 141, 145-147, 151; his retreat from Sombreffe, 66-79; his instructions and dispositions at Wavre, 108-114
Thionville, 13, 14
Thorembey les Beguignes, 9
Thuin, 9, 15, 26, 143
Tilly, 66-68, 71, 73
Tirlemont, 2
Tolly, Barclay de, 2, 4
Tongrenelles, 62
Tongres, 10
Tourinnes, 88, 99, 115, 136

UXBRIDGE, Lord, 8, 35, 39

VALENCIENNES, 12, 14
Vallin, Colonel, 136
Vandamme, General, Third Corps (French), 12, 15-18, 31, 47, 48, 57, 62, 64, 73, 85-88, 92, 94, 95, 97-99, 108, 109, 111, 134, 136, 138-140, 146, 147, 151; at Wavre, 115-119, 122, 124, 127, 129, 130, 132
Van Merlen, General, 26, 33, 34
Vervins, 146
Vichery, Colonel, 58, 127
Vieux Sart, 71, 100
Villers Perruin, 33, 49
Villets Coterets, 148-151
Vilvorde, 35

WALHAIN, 71, 92, 95, 97, 137
Warème, 10
Wavre, 44, 67-69, 72, 92-94, 98-101, 104, 106, 136; Thielemann's instructions and dispositions at, 108-114; battle of, 115-132

Wellington, Duke of, 4, 37, 38, 78, 83, 90, 93, 101; disposition of his troops in Belgium, 7; his plans, 25, 35; order for concentration, 34; a message to Blucher, 102

Wrede, Prince, 3

ZEPPELIN, Colonel, 109-111, 113, 129, 132

Zieten, General, First Corps (Prussian), 8-10, 17, 22, 25-29, 31, 32, 34, 35, 66-68, 70, 72, 73, 100, 103, 106, 114, 125, 142, 143, 145, 146-151

www.ingramcontent.com/pod-product-compliance
Lightning Source LLC
Chambersburg PA
CBHW061141230426
43663CB00028B/2994